Dinosaur Cross Stitch Charts

Allosaurus
Aptosaurus
Pteranodon
Spinosaurus
Stegosaurus
Styracosaurus
Triceratops
T-rex

ABOUT THE PATTERNS

Choose canvas and threads to create your own unique dinosaur designs. Stitch in pastel colors to create wall art for a nursery, stitch in black to create a stunning piece of decor or try some variagated threads for something a little different.

You will find two versions of each dinosaur design (100 & 200 stitches wide) to allow you to chose the detail level you require.

The measurements given on each dinosaur preview page are for guidance, and assume 14 stitches per inch.

Where charts are split over multiple pages, you will see we have included an overlap of two rows of stitches. They are shown in the pattern with a grayed out back-ground and should not be stitched again but used to match up the next page of stitches.

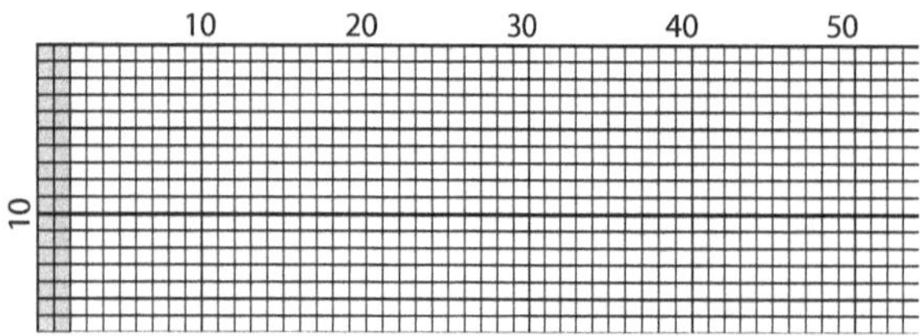

Allosaurous - page 1

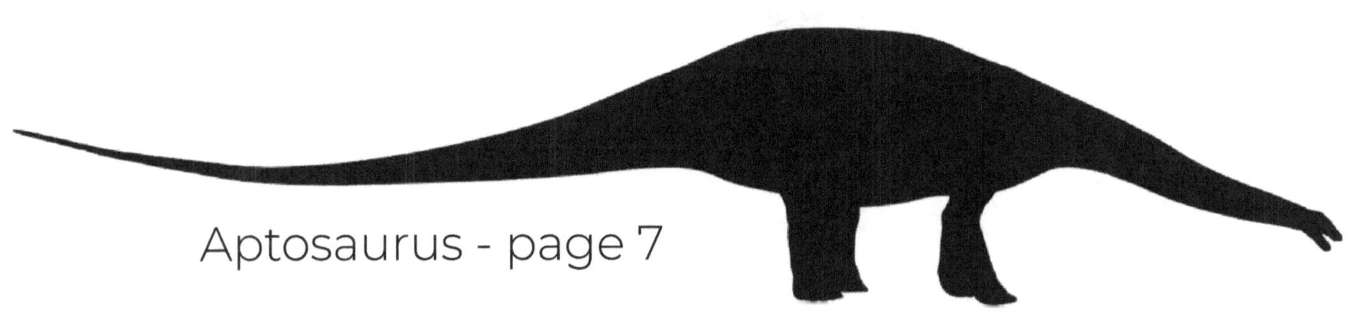

Aptosaurus - page 7

Pteranodon - page 13

Spinosaurus - page 19

Stegosaurus

Styracosaurus - page 35

Triceratops - page 43

T-rex page 49

Allosaurus

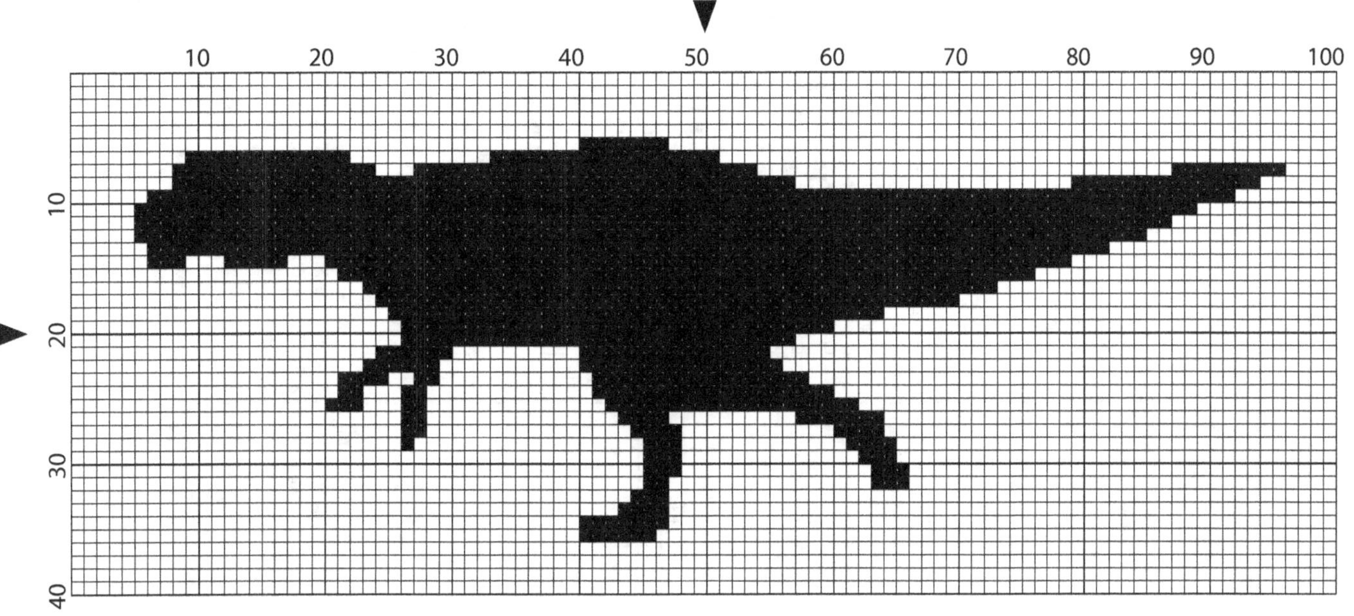

Grid Size:	100W x 40H
Design Area:	6.57" x 2.21" (92 x 31 stitches)

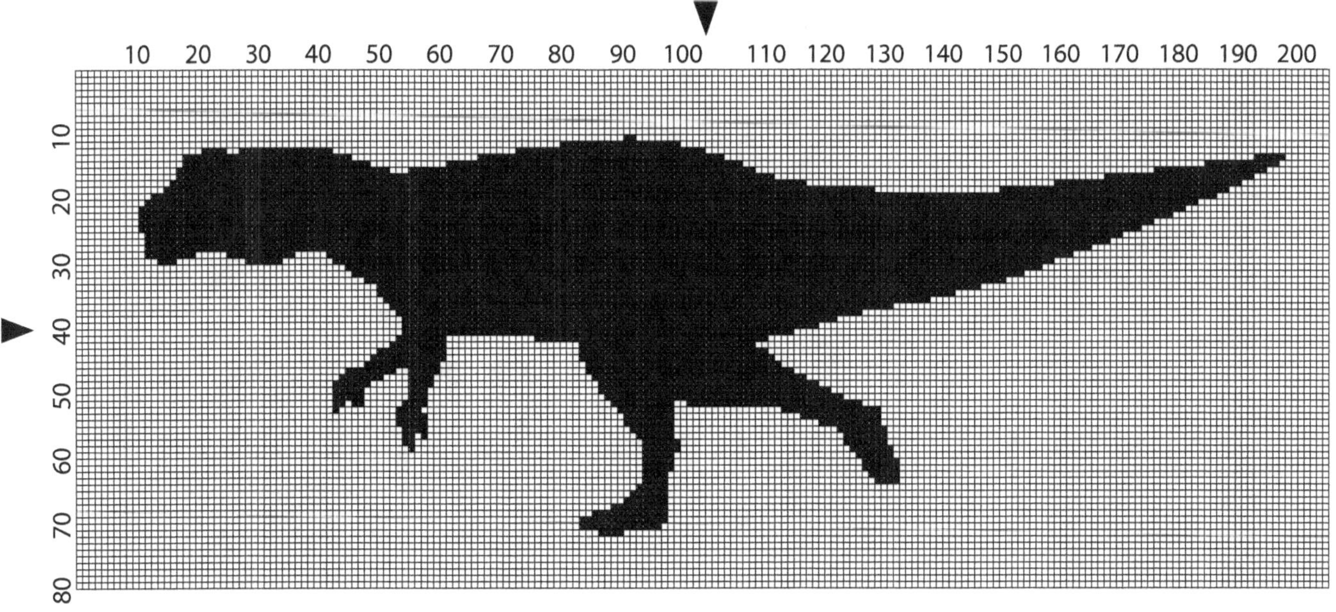

Grid Size:	200W x 80H
Design Area:	13.07" x 4.43" (183 x 62 stitches)

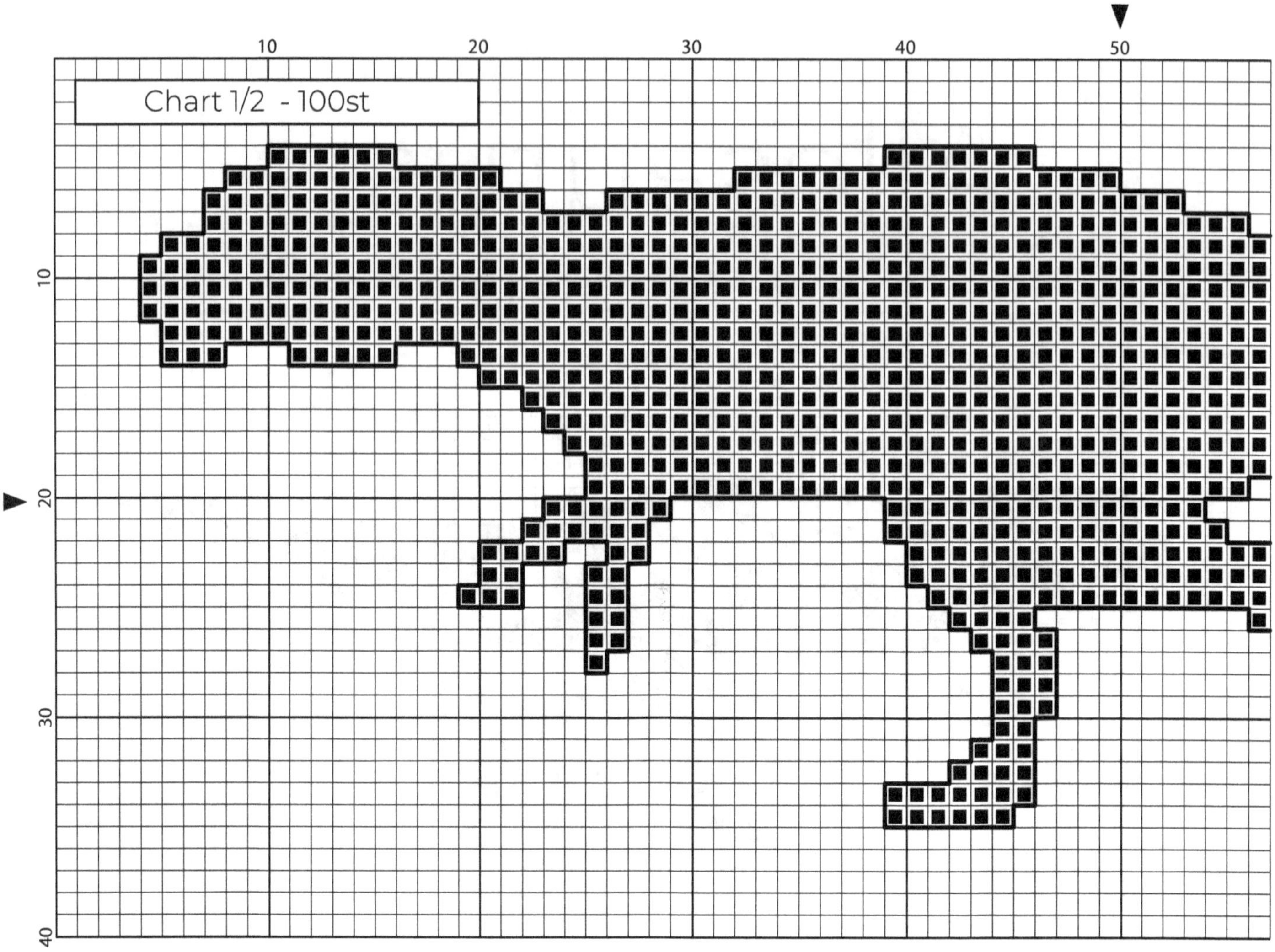

Chart 1/2 - 100st

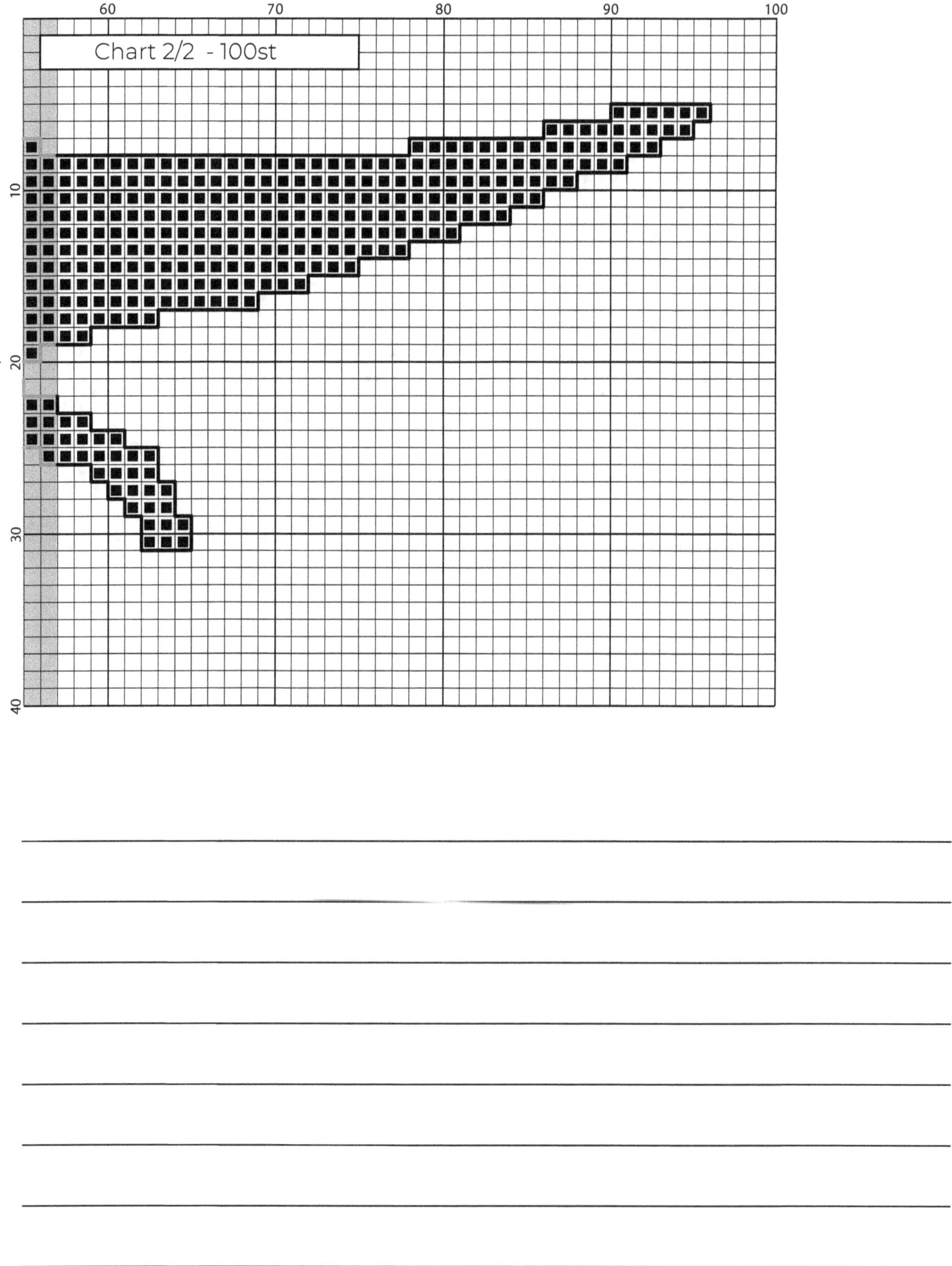

Chart 2/2 - 100st

Chart 1/3 - 200st

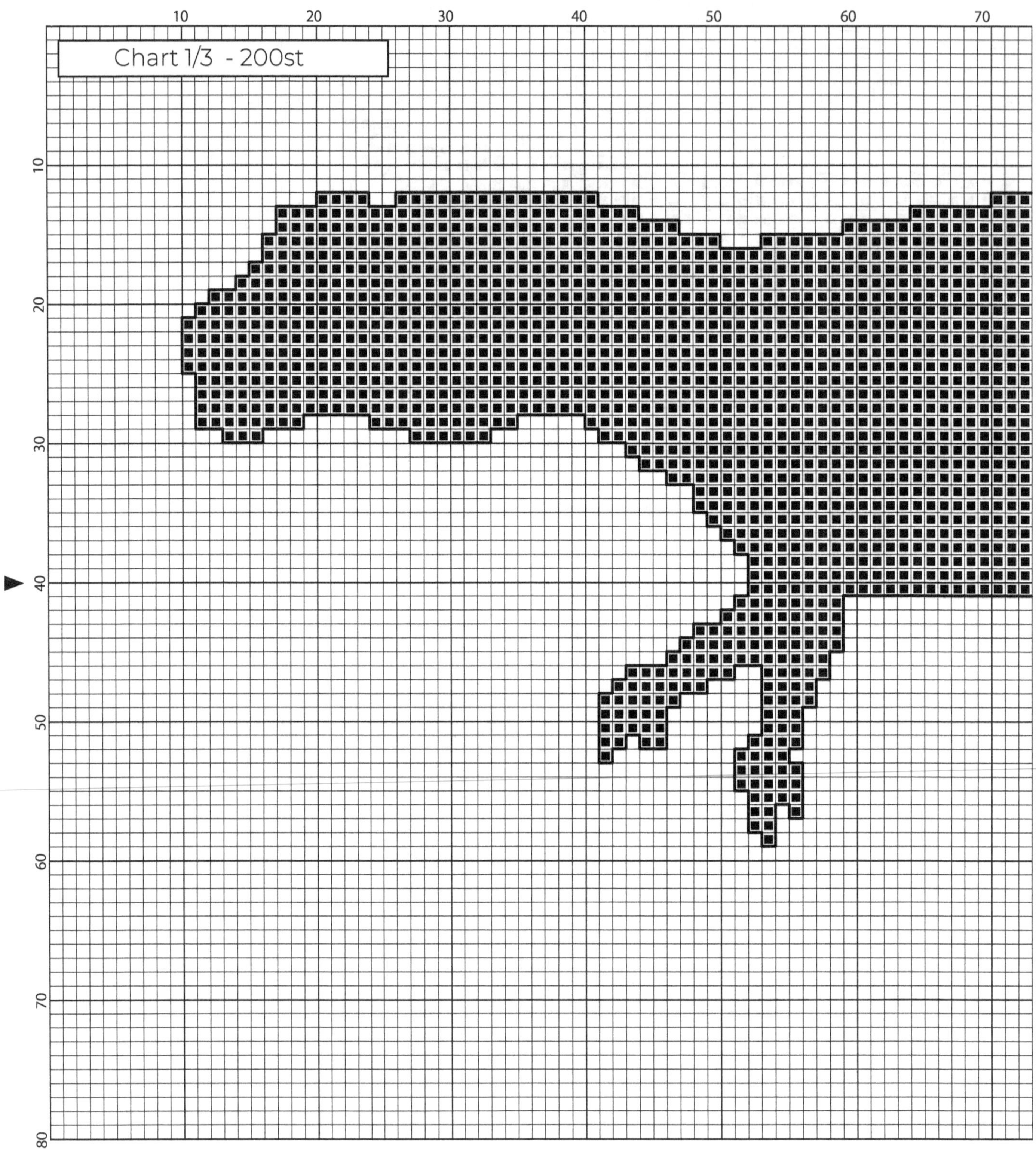

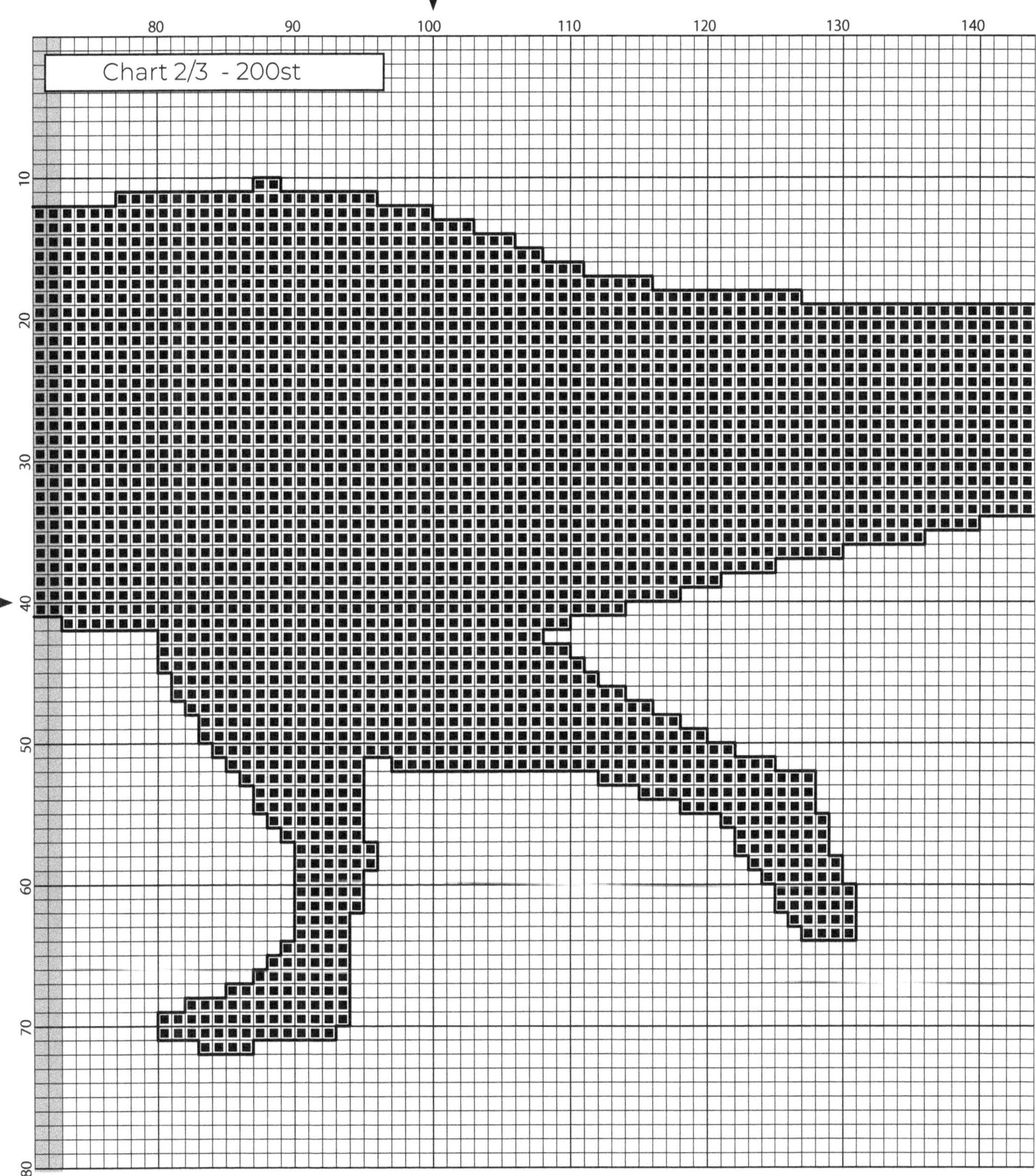

Chart 2/3 - 200st

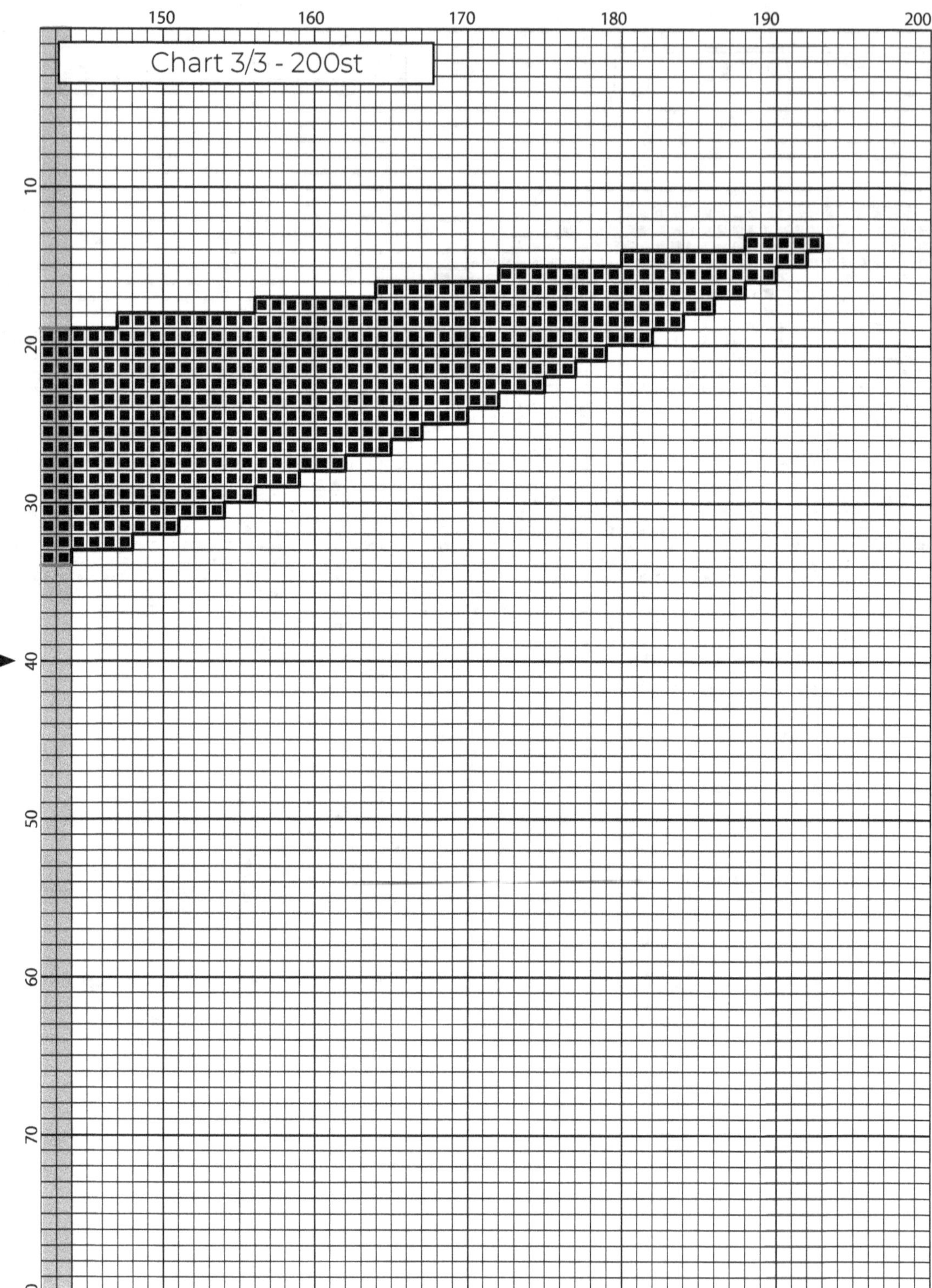

150
160
170
180
190
200
Chart 3/3 - 200st
10
20
30
40
50
60
70
80

Apatosaurus

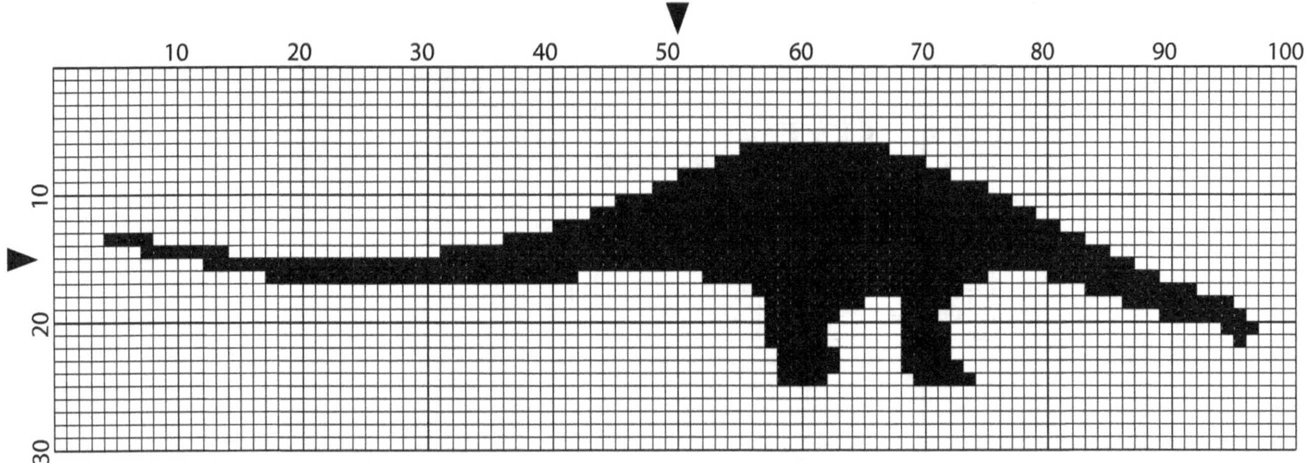

Grid Size: 100W x 30H
Design Area: 6.64" x 1.36" (93 x 19 stitches)

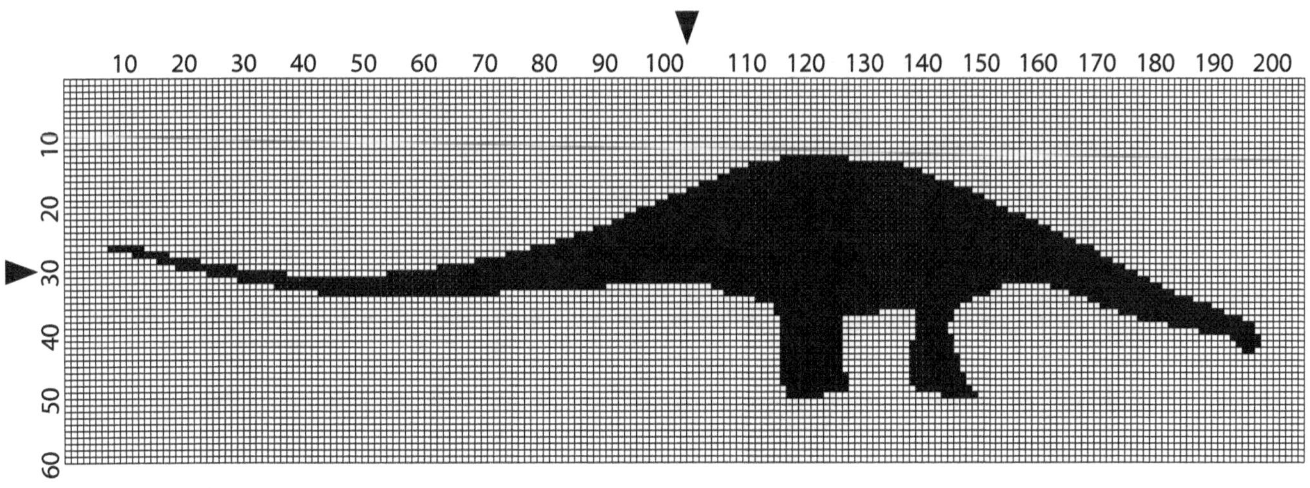

Grid Size: 200W x 60H
Design Area: 13.29" x 2.71" (186 x 38 stitches)

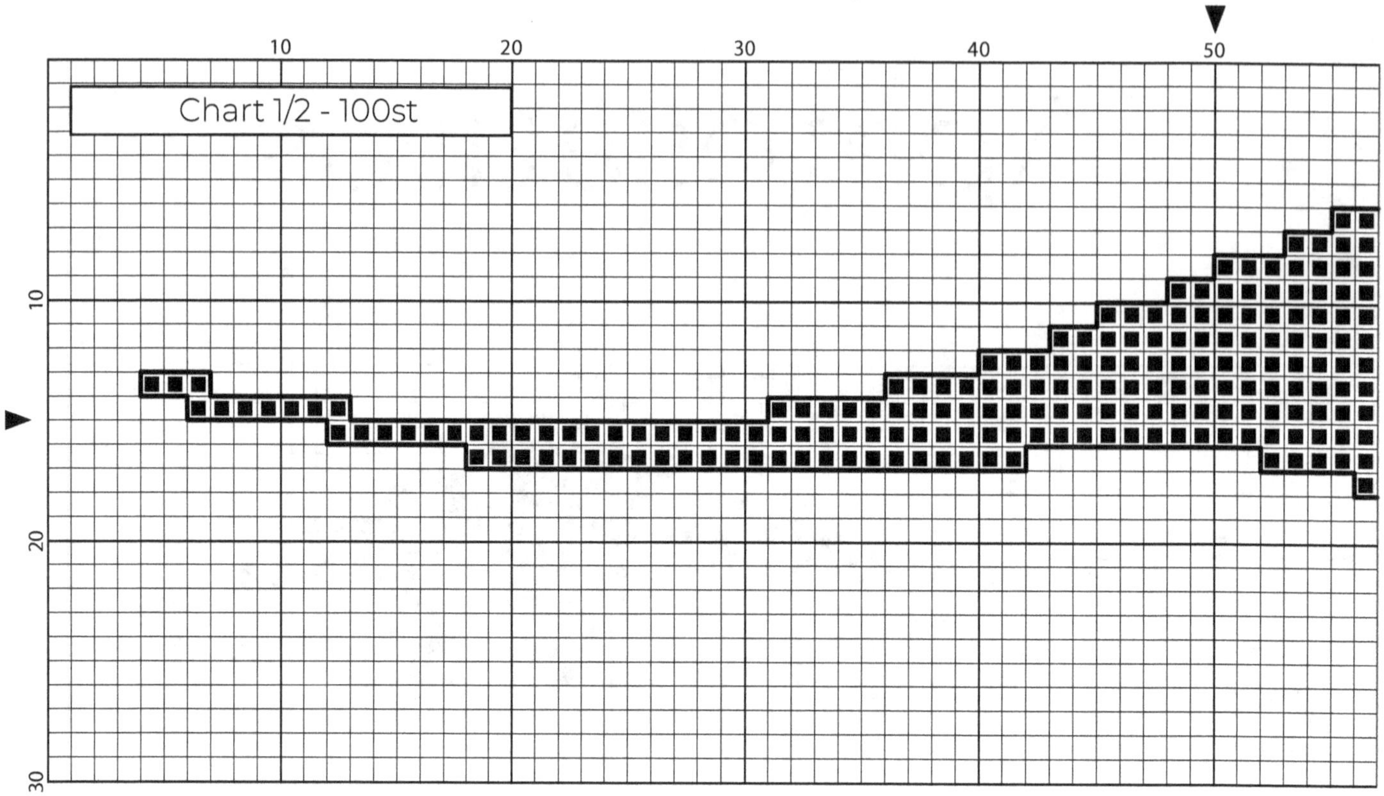

Chart 1/2 - 100st
10
20
30
40
50
10
20
30

60
70
80
90
100
Chart 2/2 - 100st

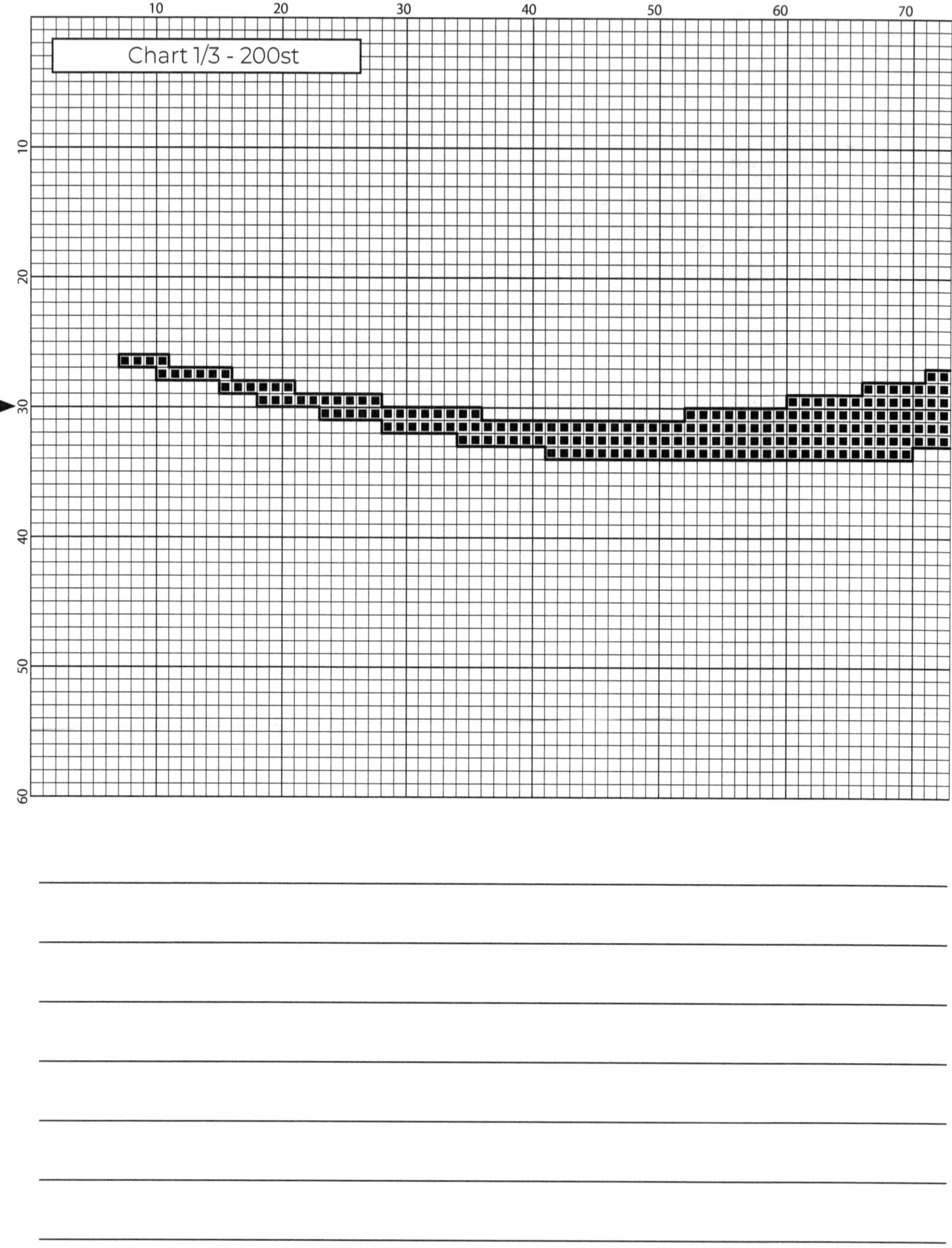
Chart 1/3 - 200st

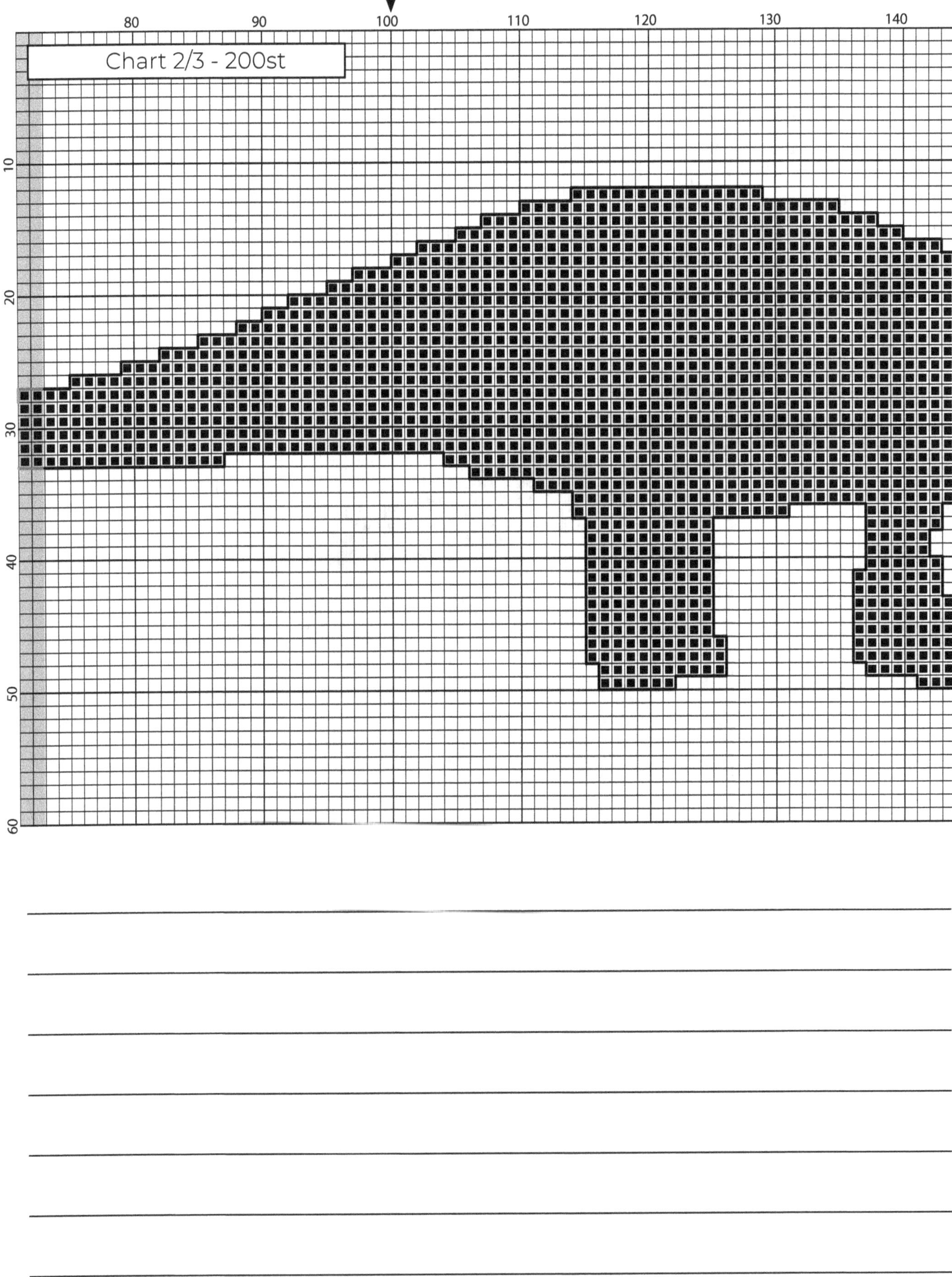

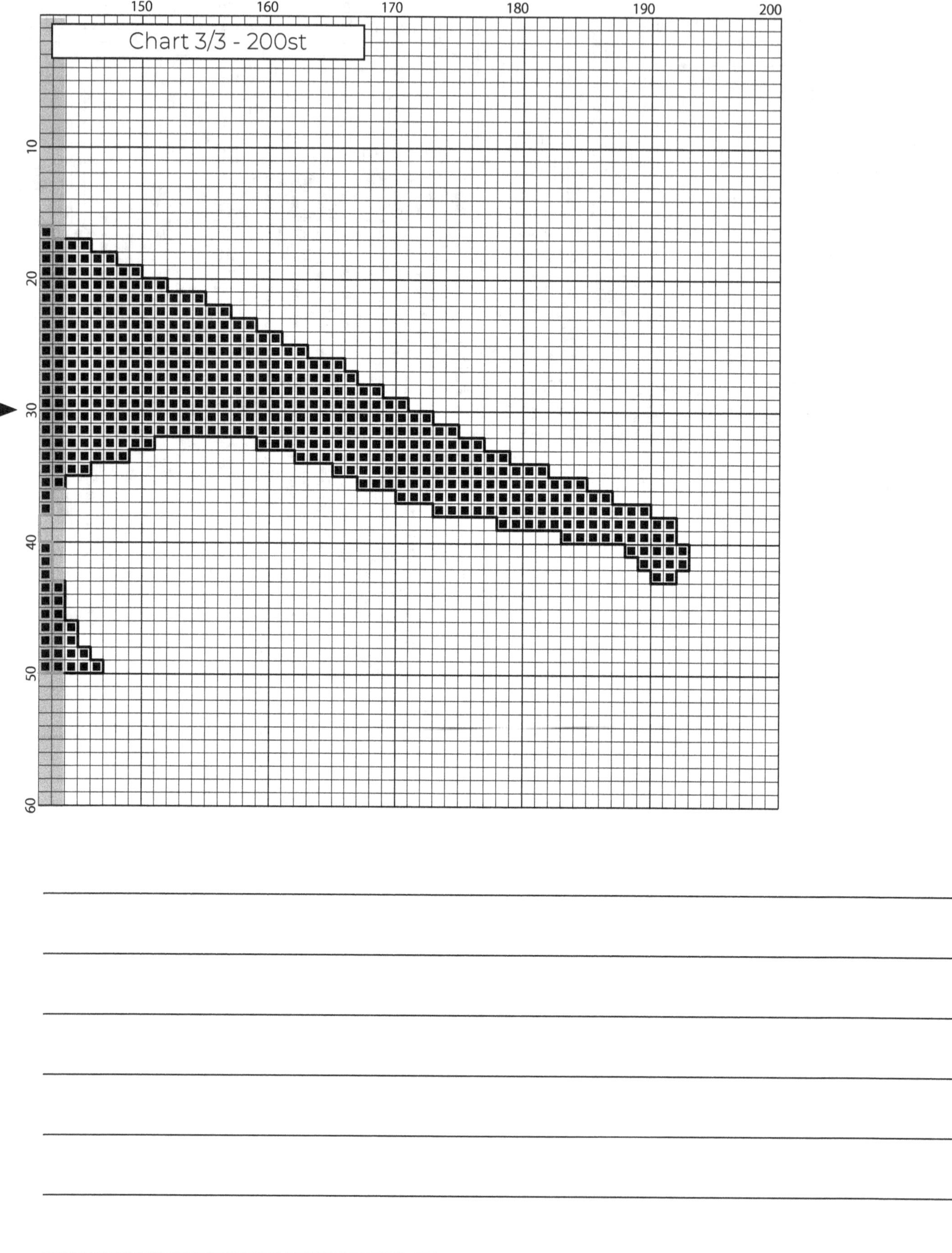

Chart 3/3 - 200st
150
160
170
180
190
200
10
20
30
40
50
60

Pteranodon

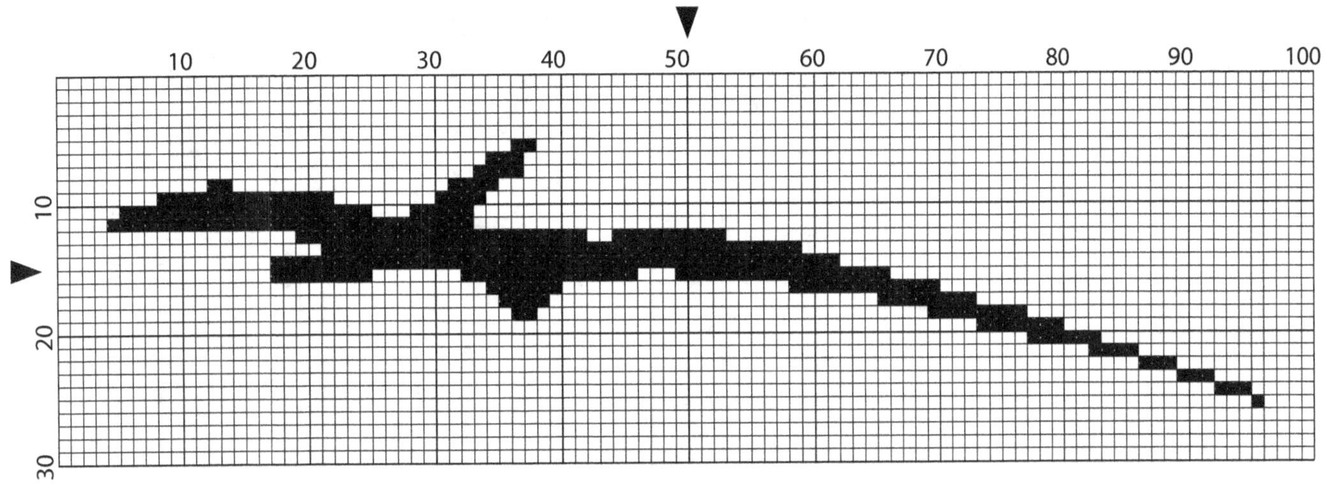

Grid Size: 100W x 30H
Design Area: 6.57" x 1.50" (92 x 21 stitches)

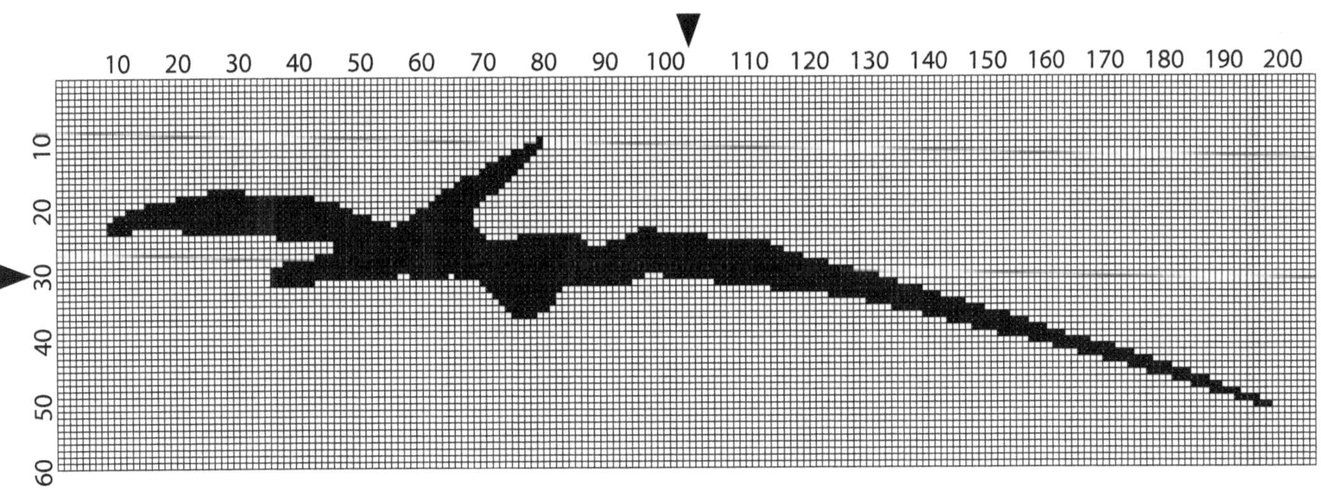

Grid Size: 200W x 60H
Design Area: 13.21" x 3.00" (185 x 42 stitches)

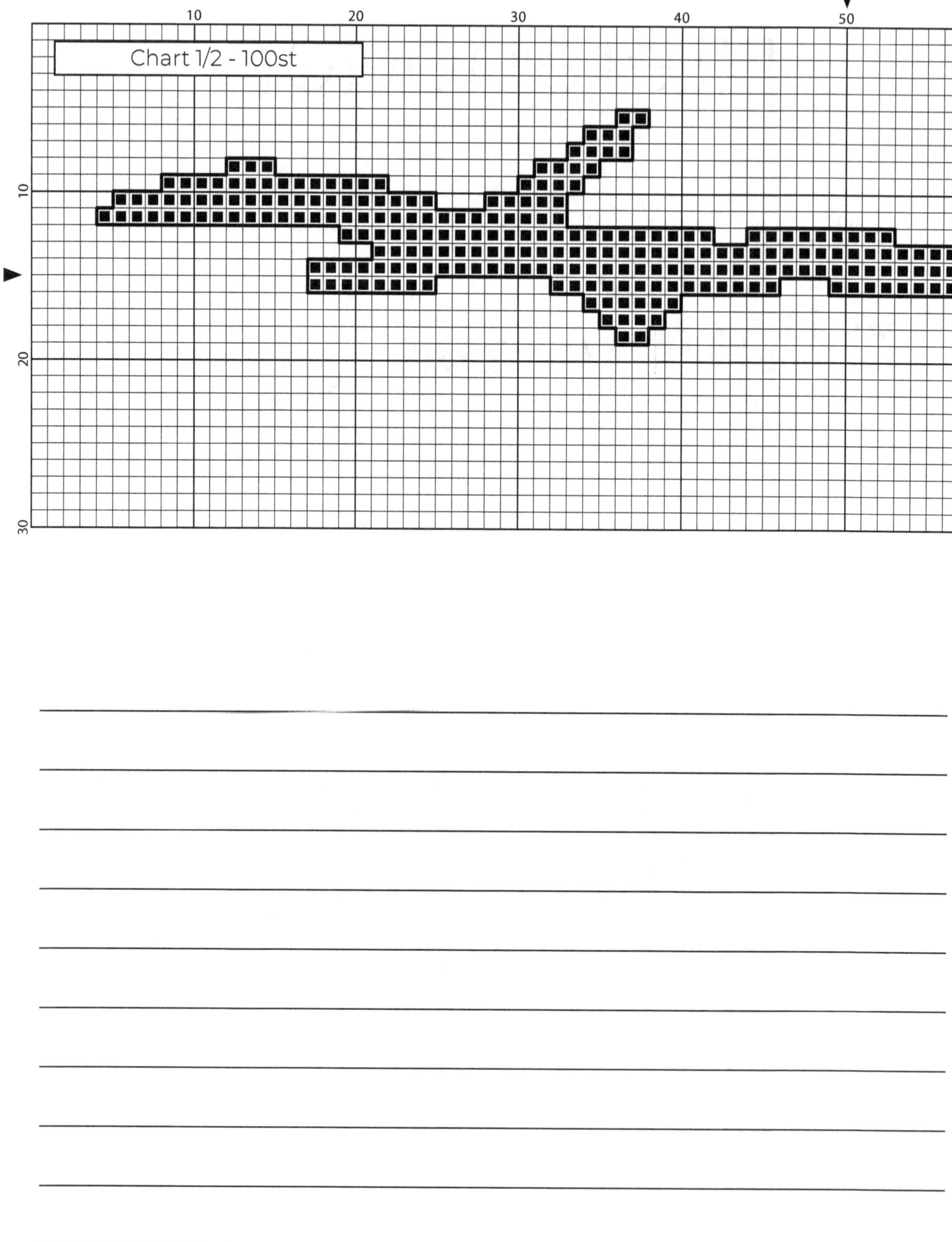

Chart 1/2 - 100st
10
20
30
40
50
10
20
30

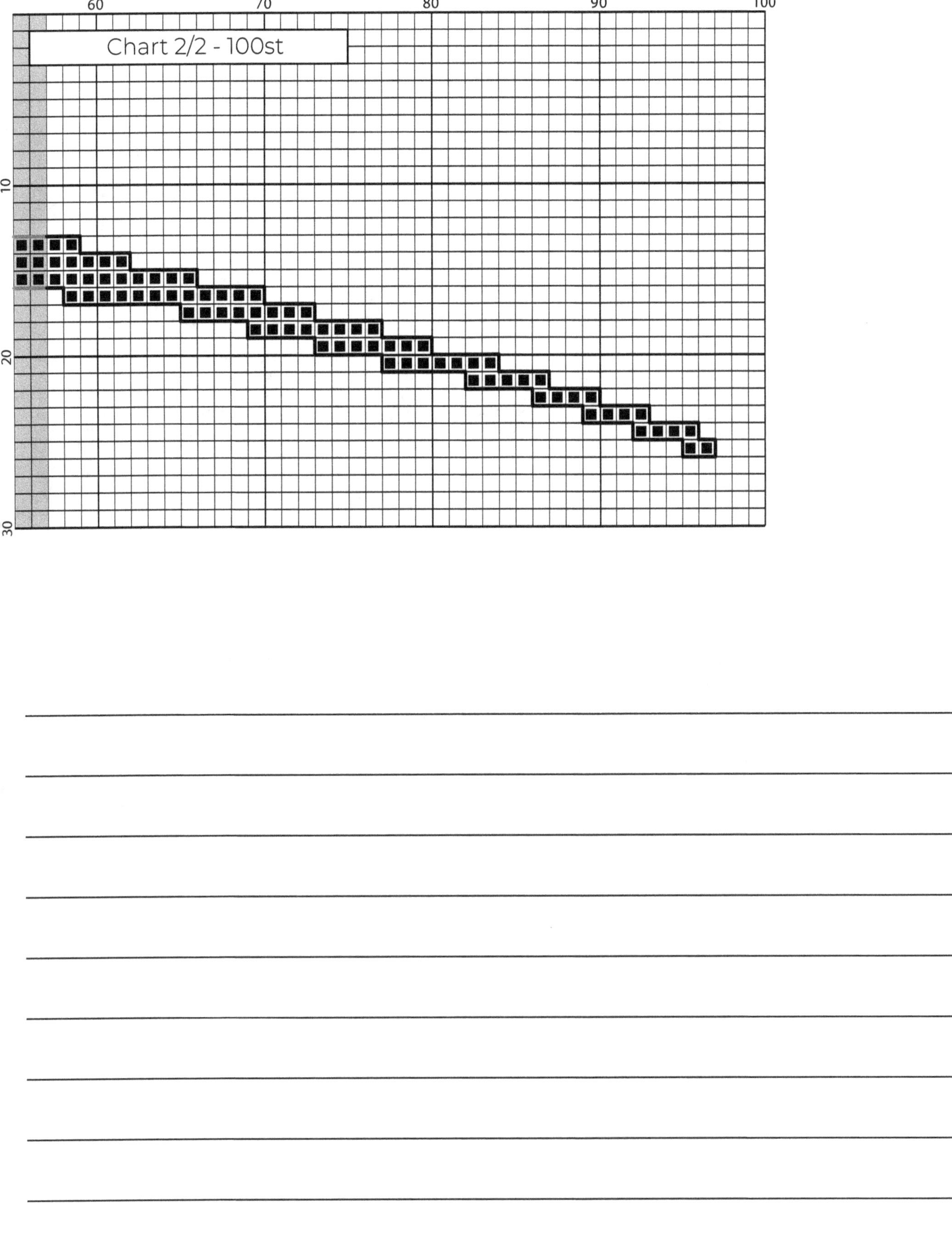

Chart 2/2 - 100st

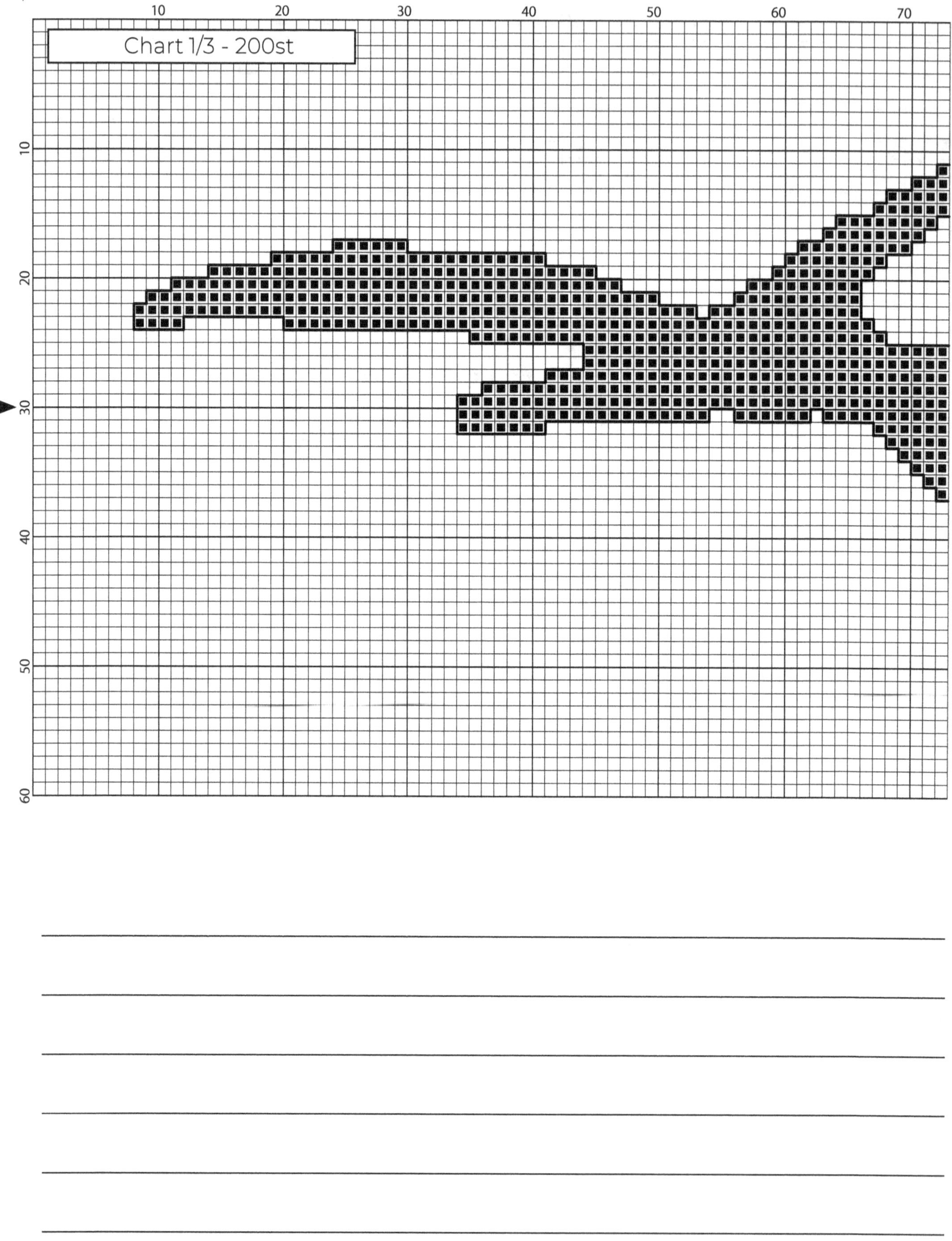
Chart 1/3 - 200st

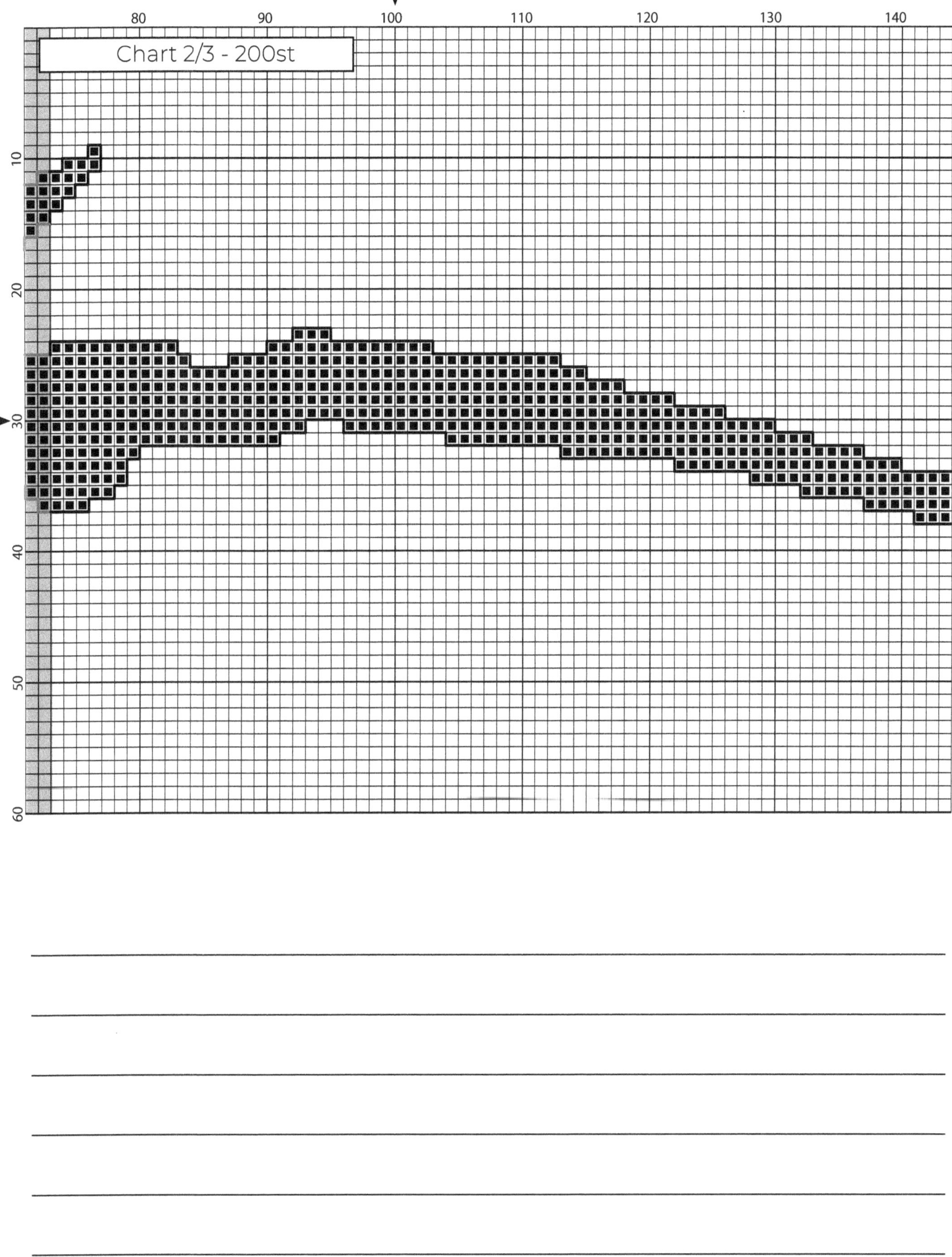

Chart 2/3 - 200st
80   90   100   110   120   130   140
10
20
30
40
50
60

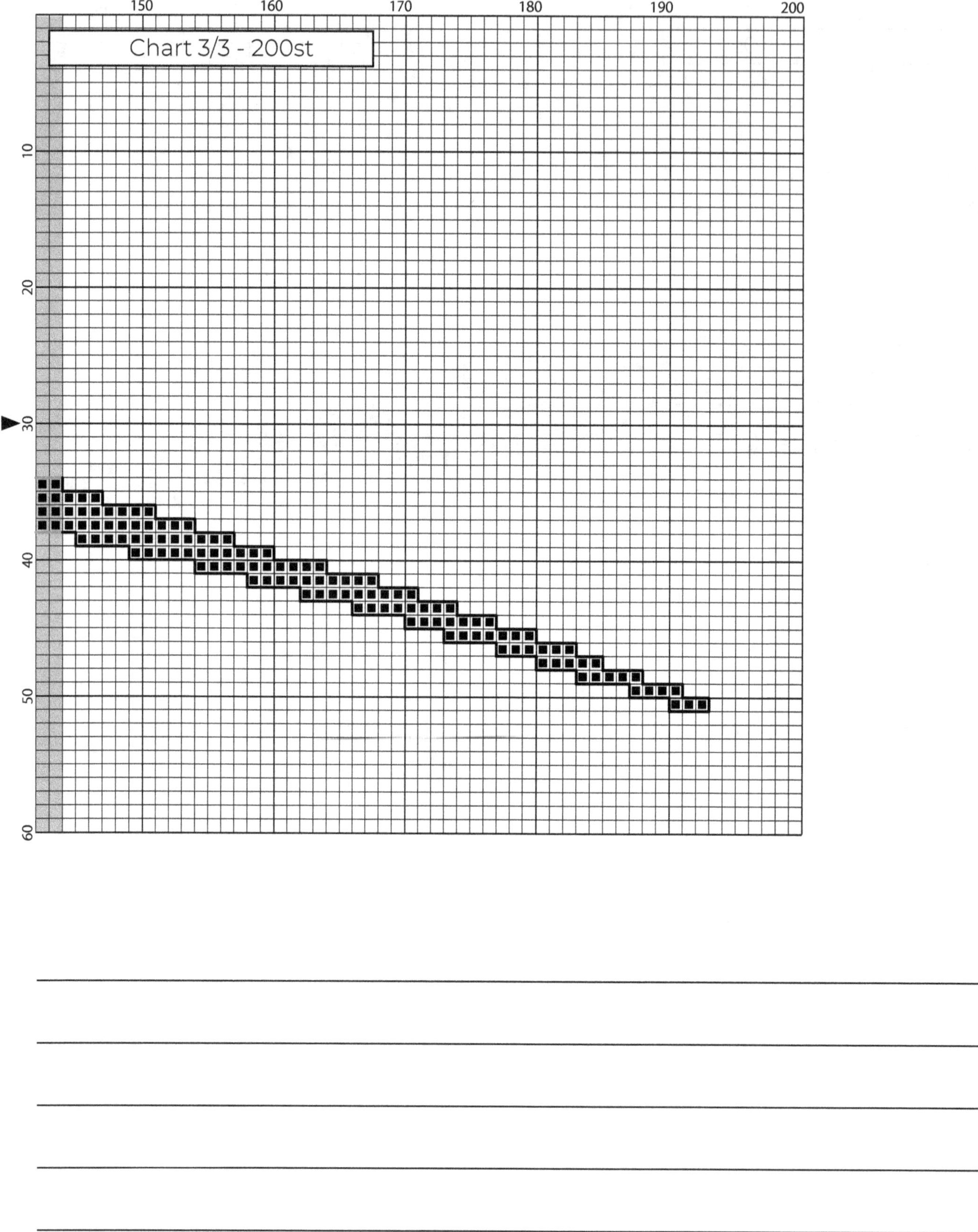

Chart 3/3 - 200st
150
160
170
180
190
200
10
20
30
40
50
60

Spinosaurus

Grid Size: 100W x 70H
Design Area: 6.50" x 4.00" (91 x 56 stitches)

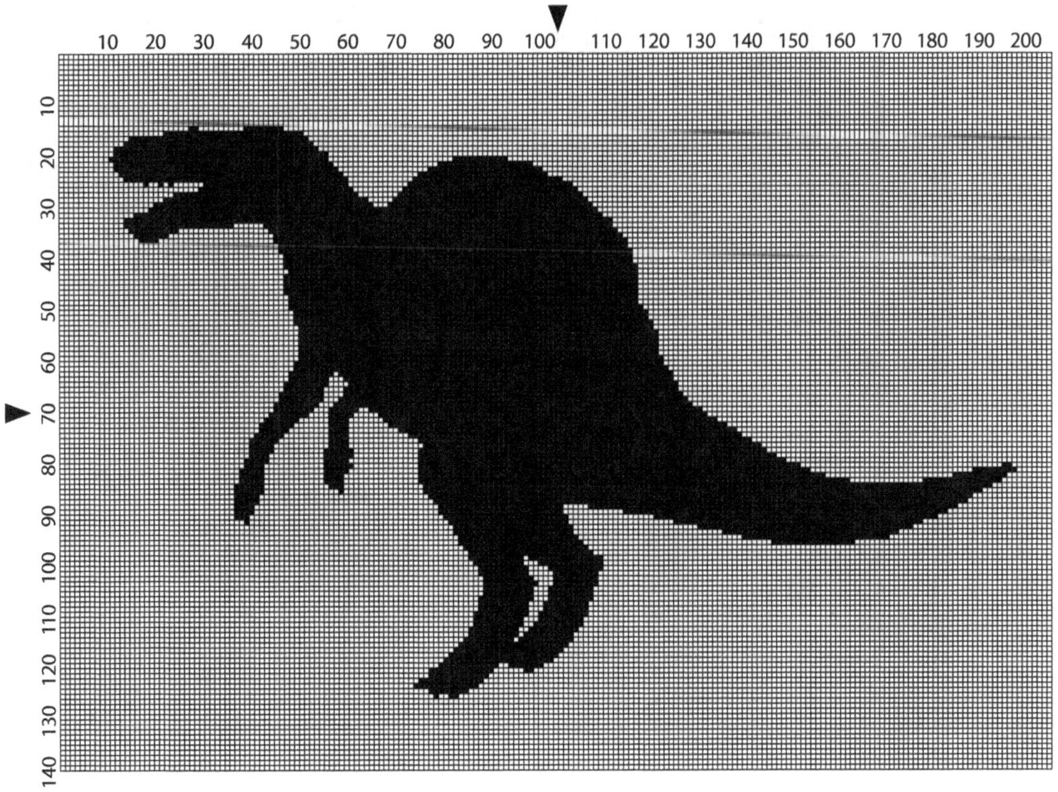

Grid Size: 200W x 140H
Design Area: 13.07" x 8.00" (183 x 112 stitches)

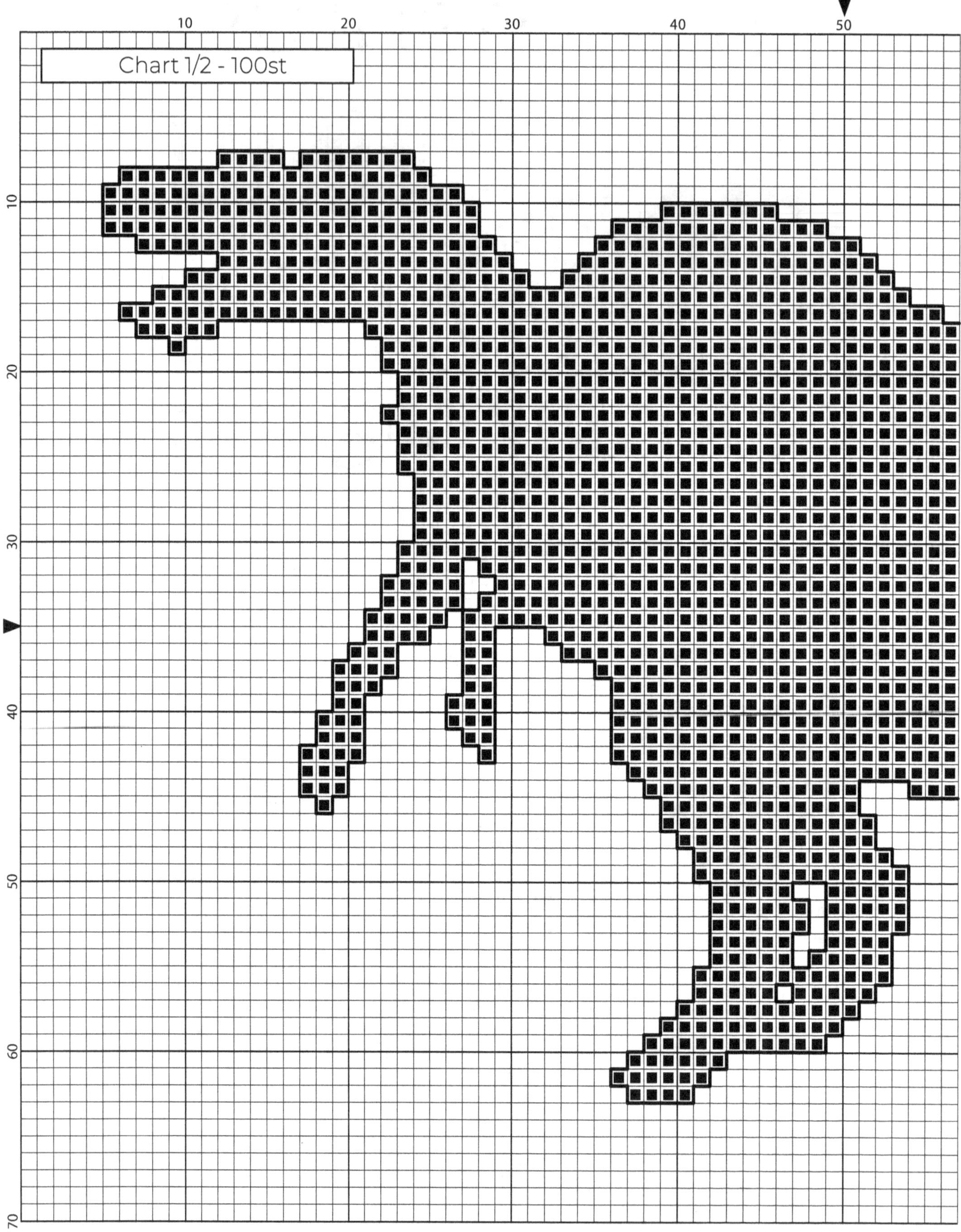

20

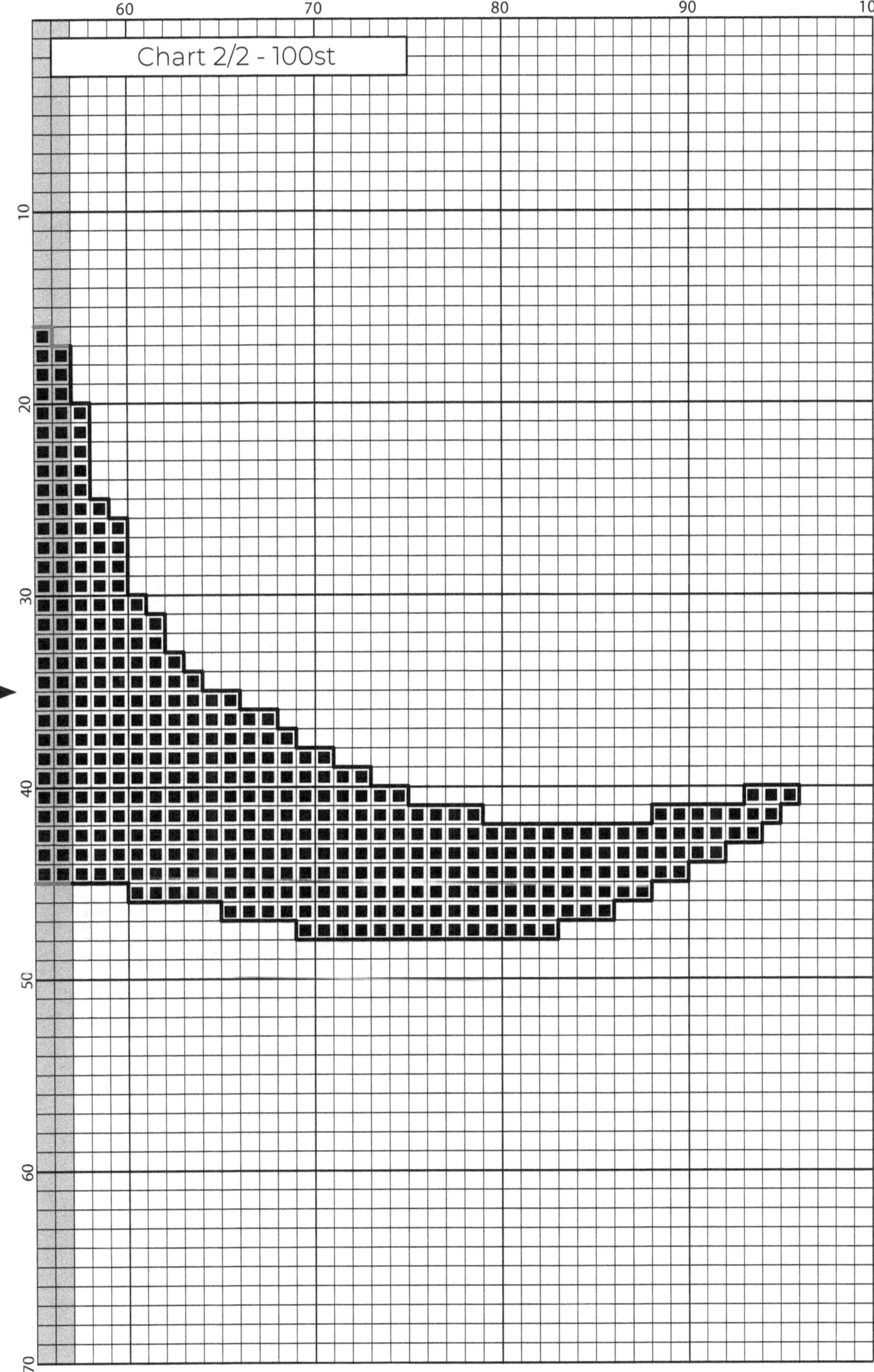

Chart 2/2 - 100st

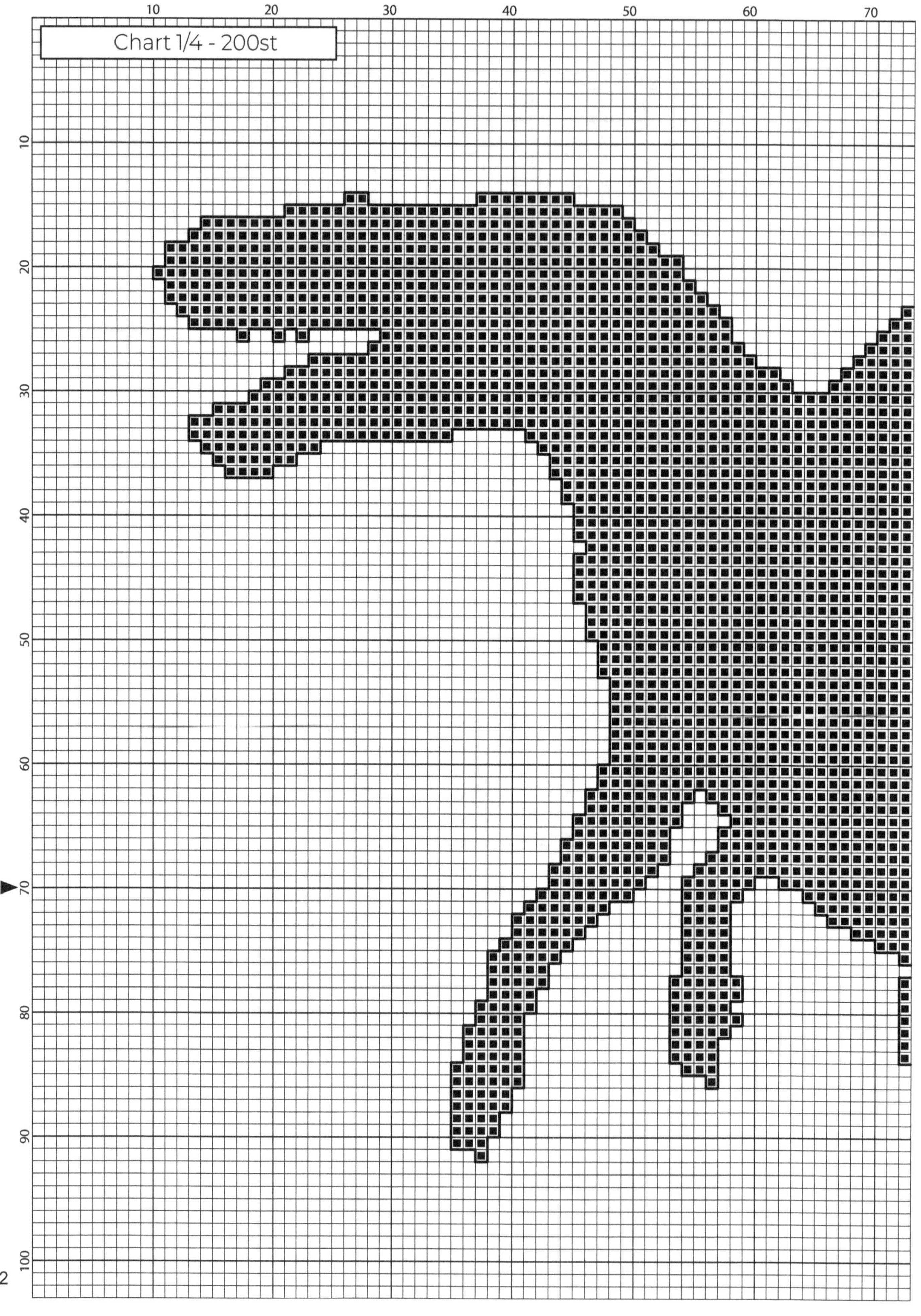

22

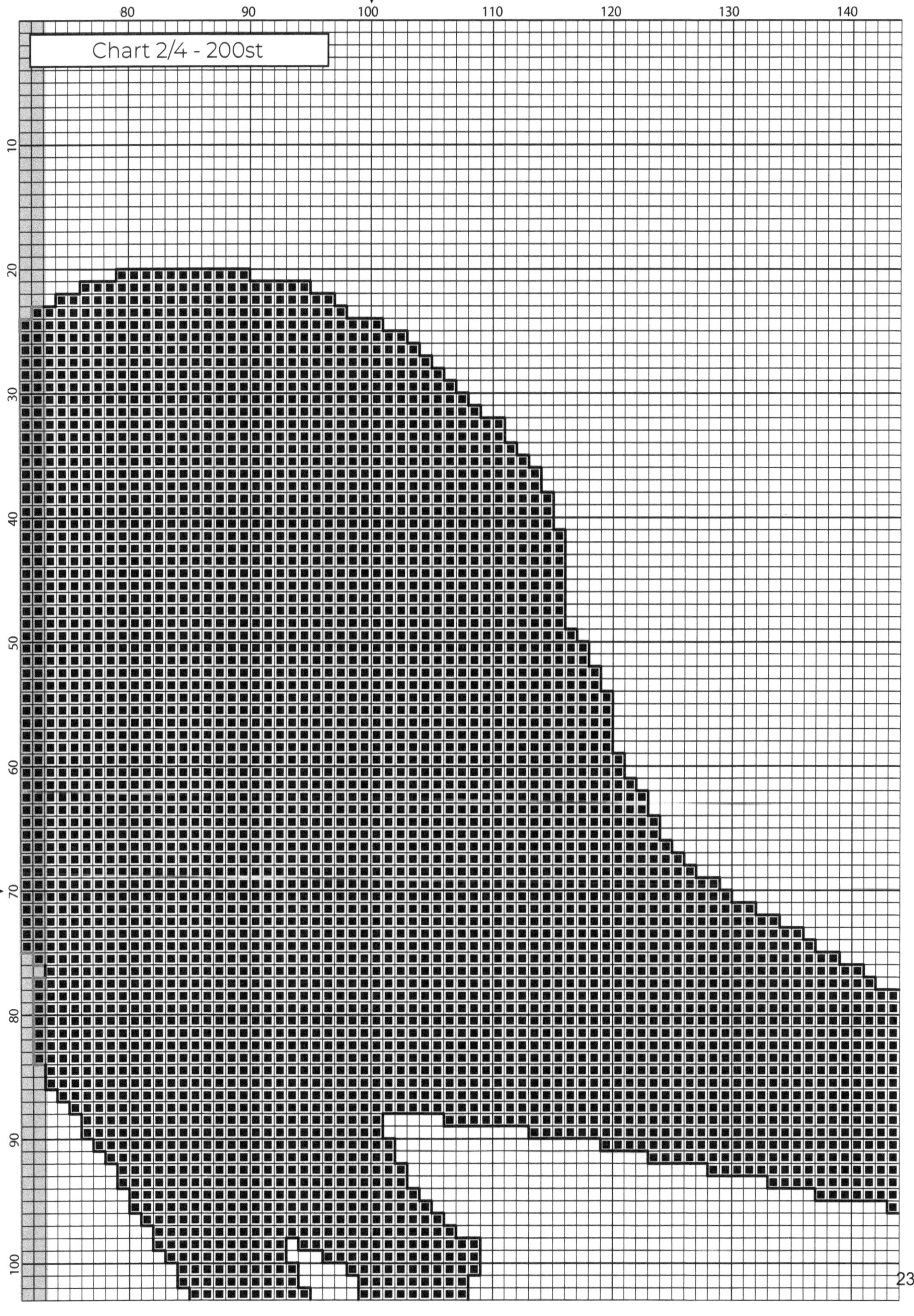

Chart 2/4 - 200st
23

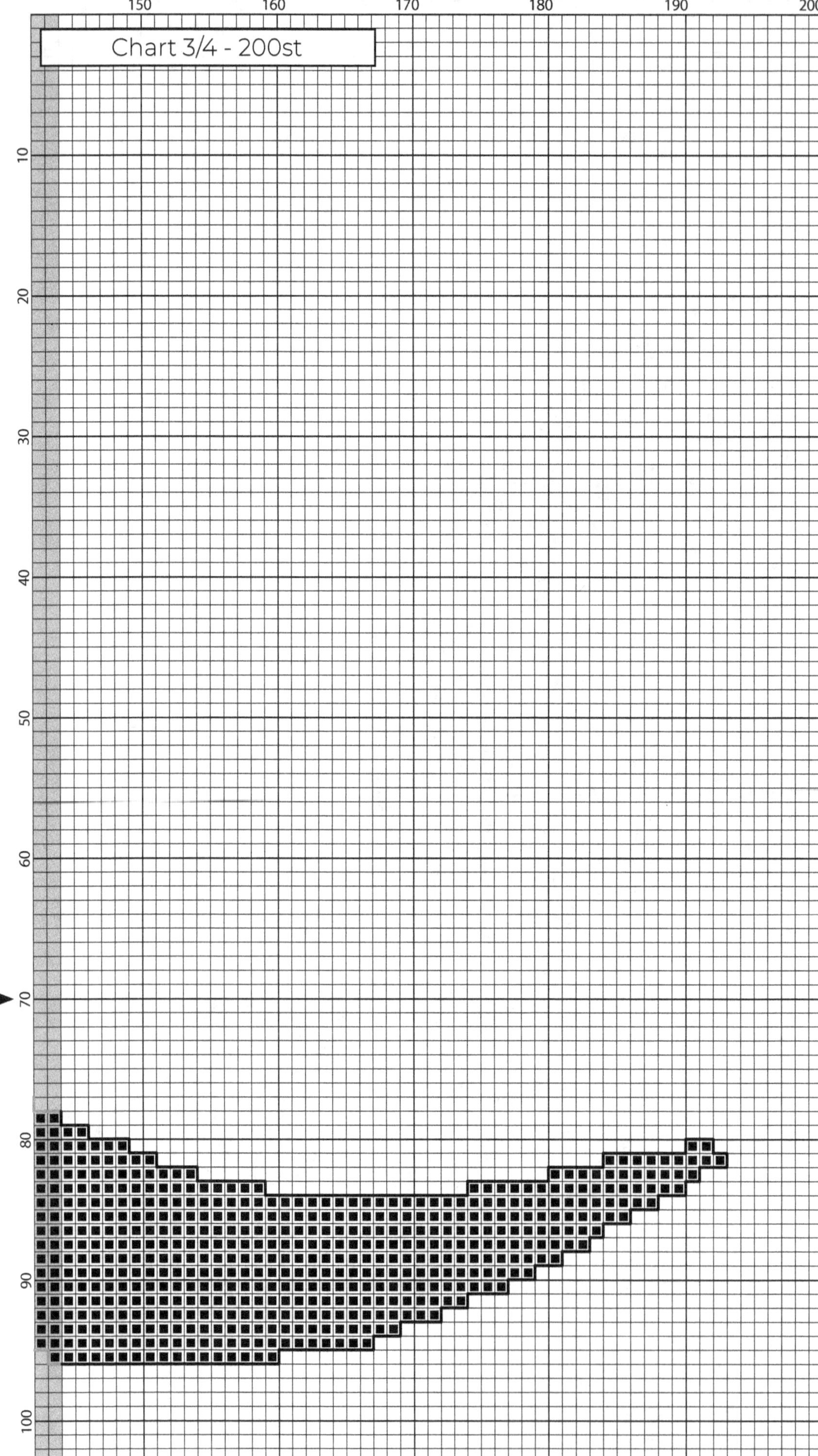

Chart 3/4 - 200st

Chart 4/4 - 200st

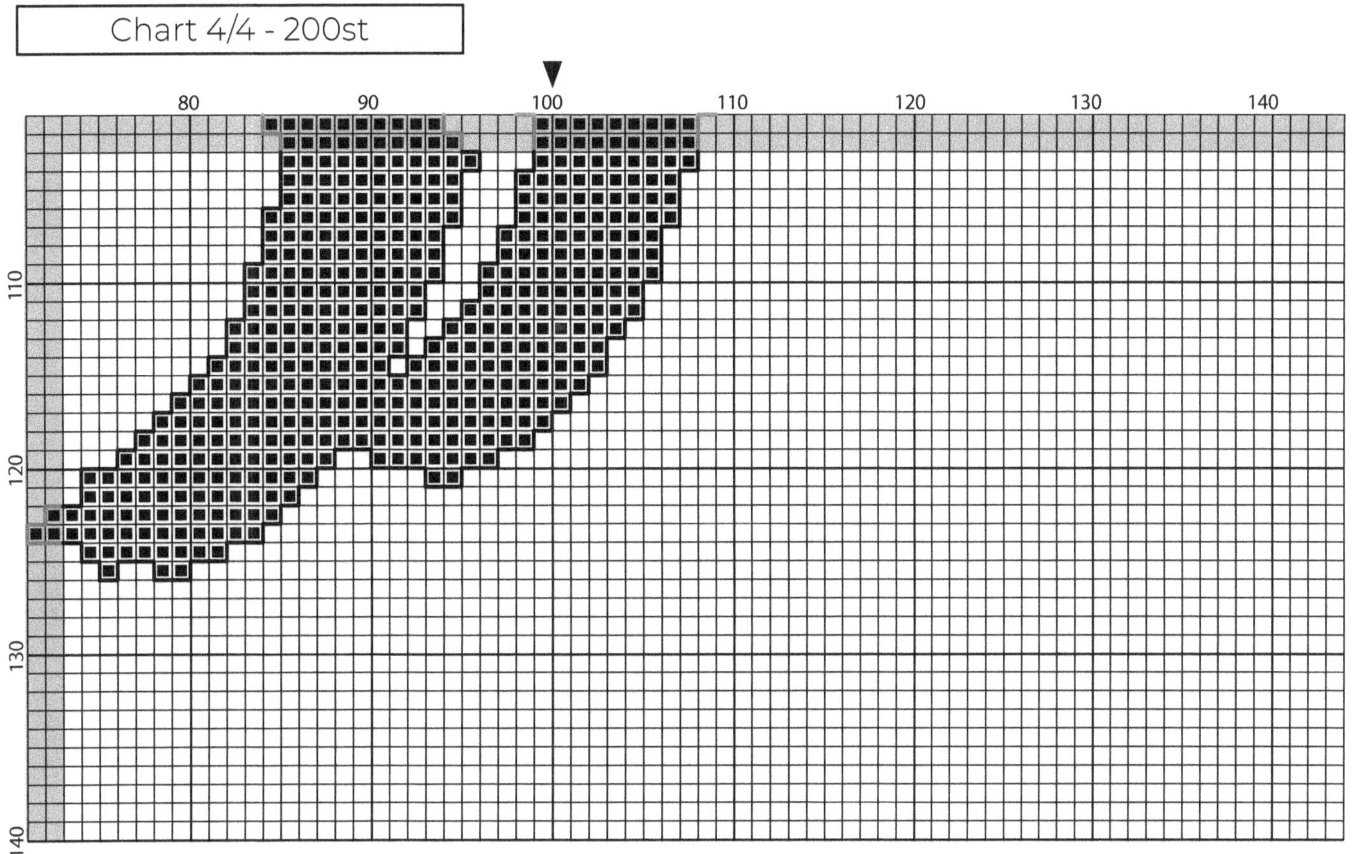

Stegosaurus

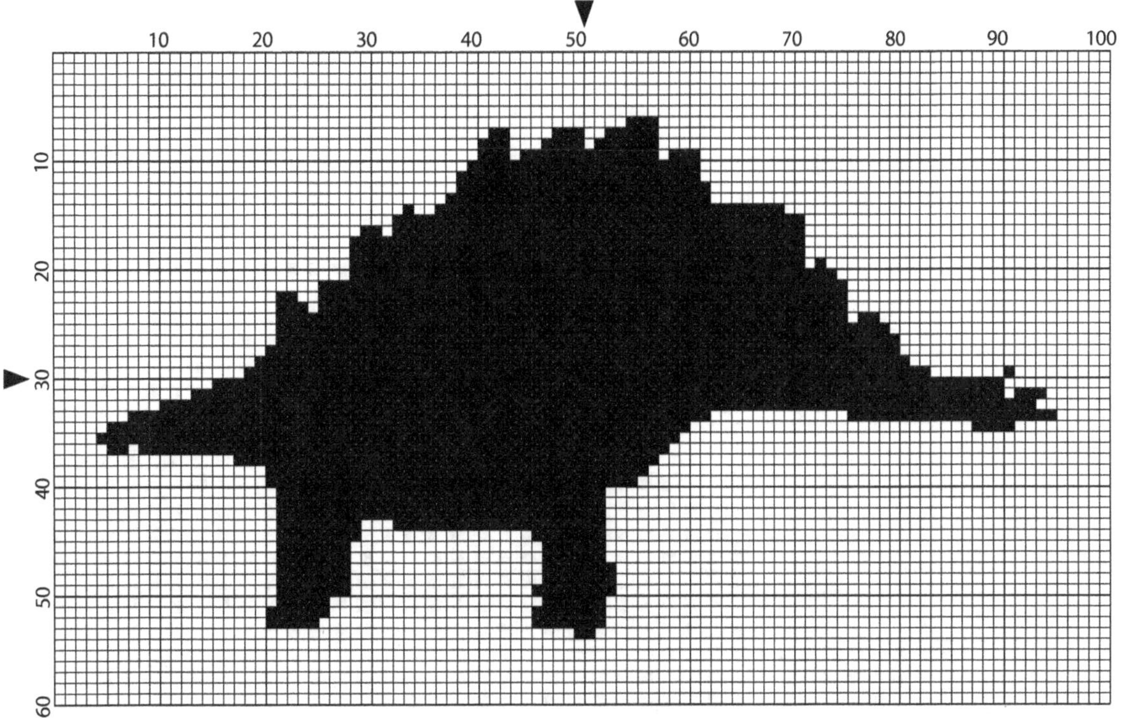

Grid Size: 100W x 60H
Design Area: 6.50" x 3.43" (91 x 48 stitches)

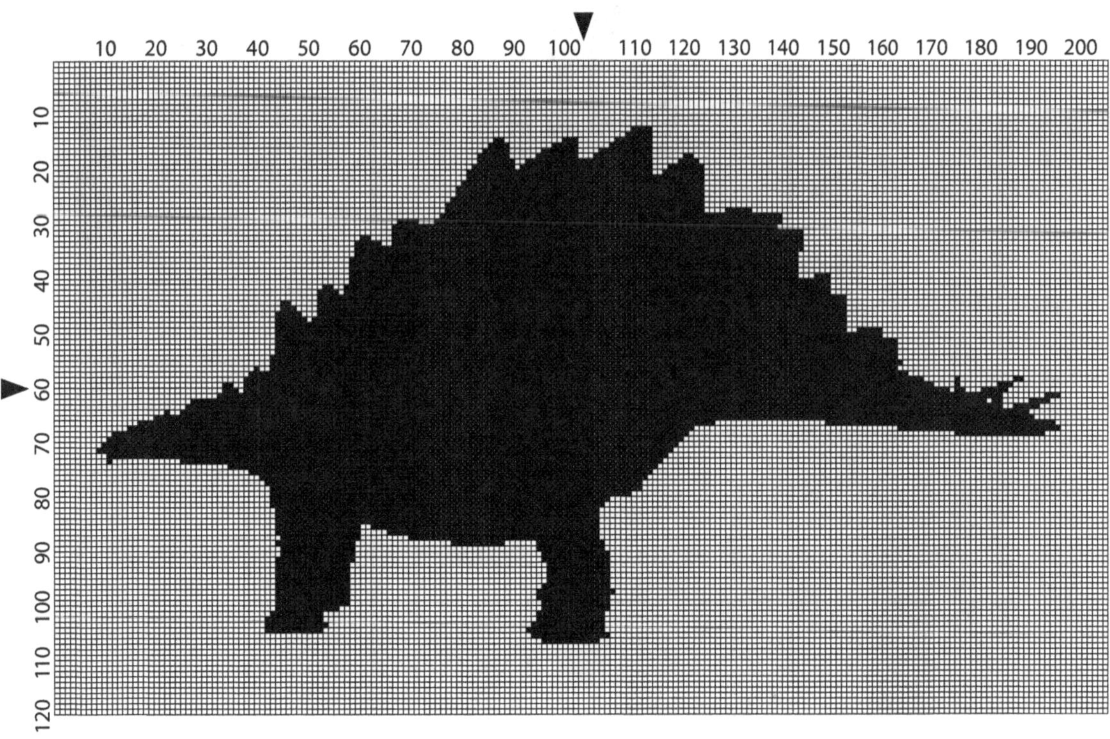

Grid Size: 200W x 120H
Design Area: 13.07" x 6.79" (183 x 95 stitches)

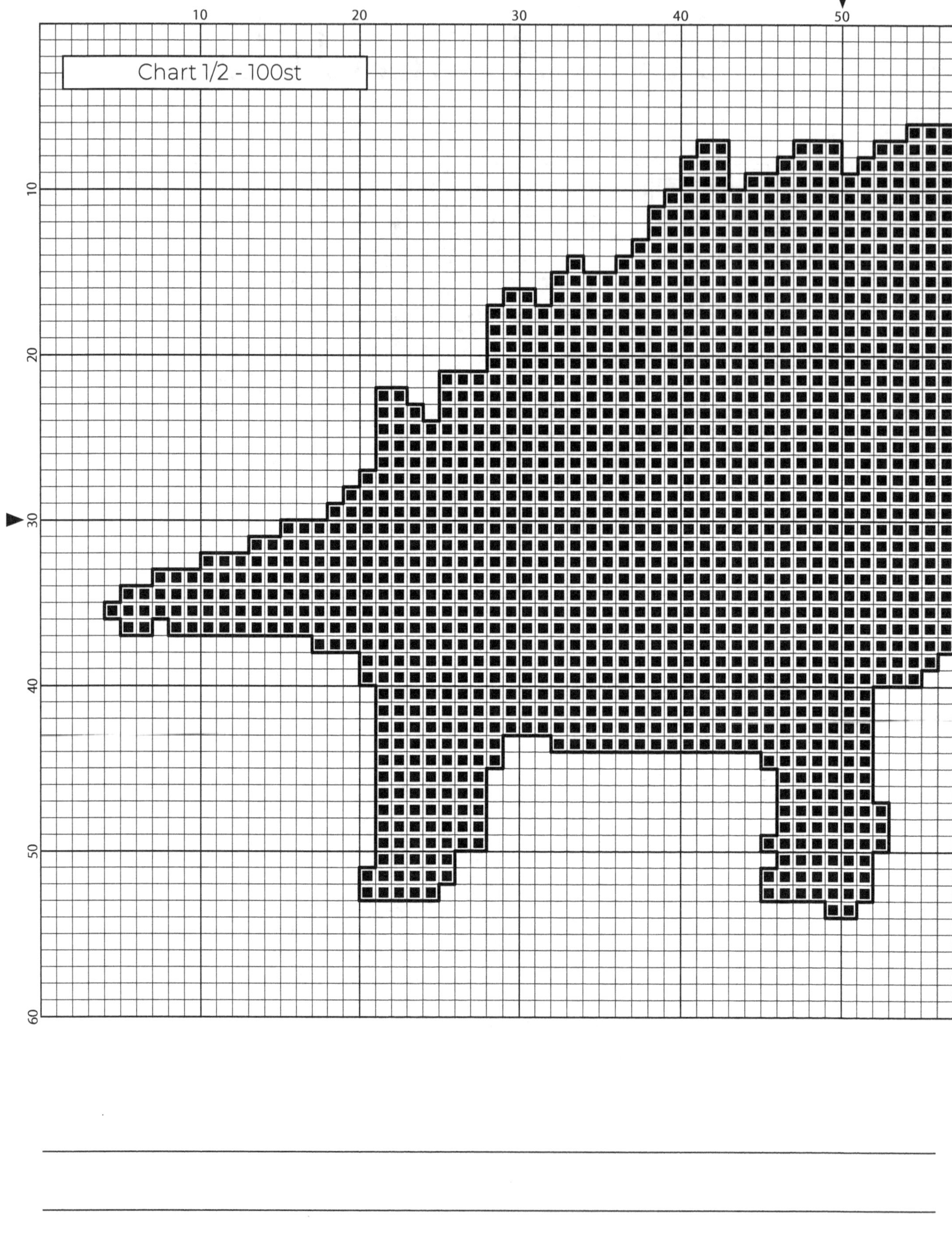

Chart 1/2 - 100st
10
20
30
40
50
10
20
30
40
50
60

60   70   80   90   100
10
20
30
40
50
60
Chart 2/2 - 100st

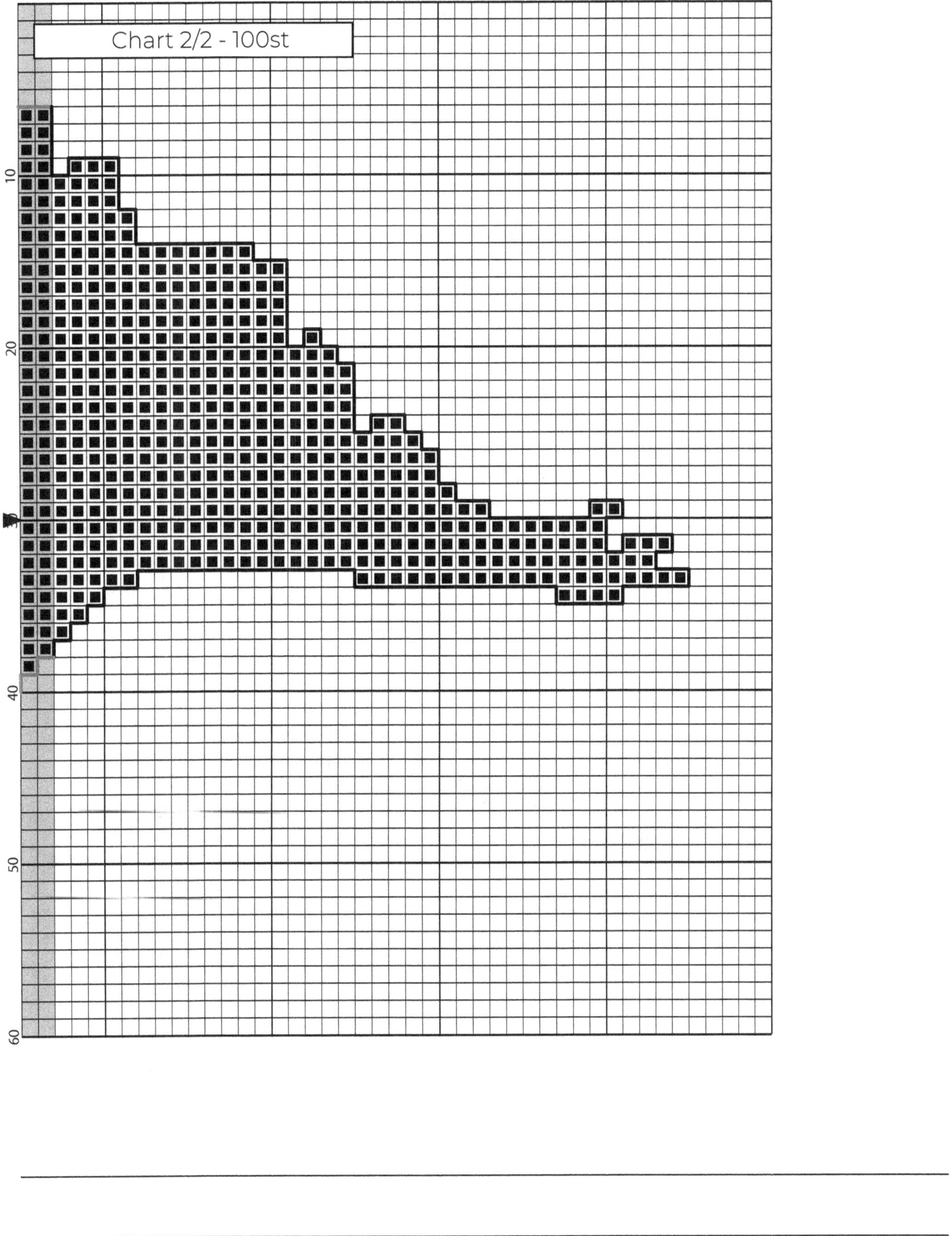

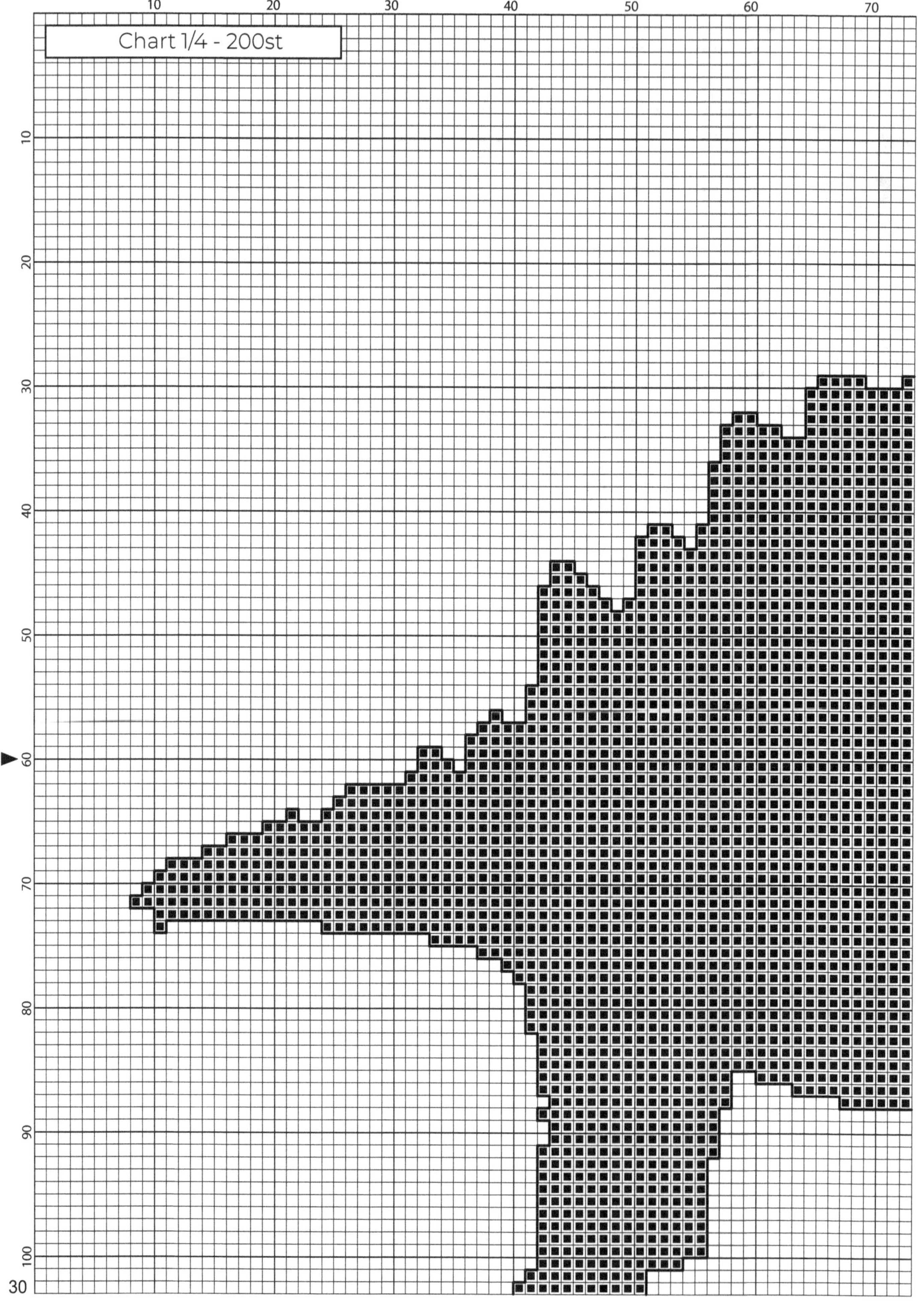
Chart 1/4 - 200st

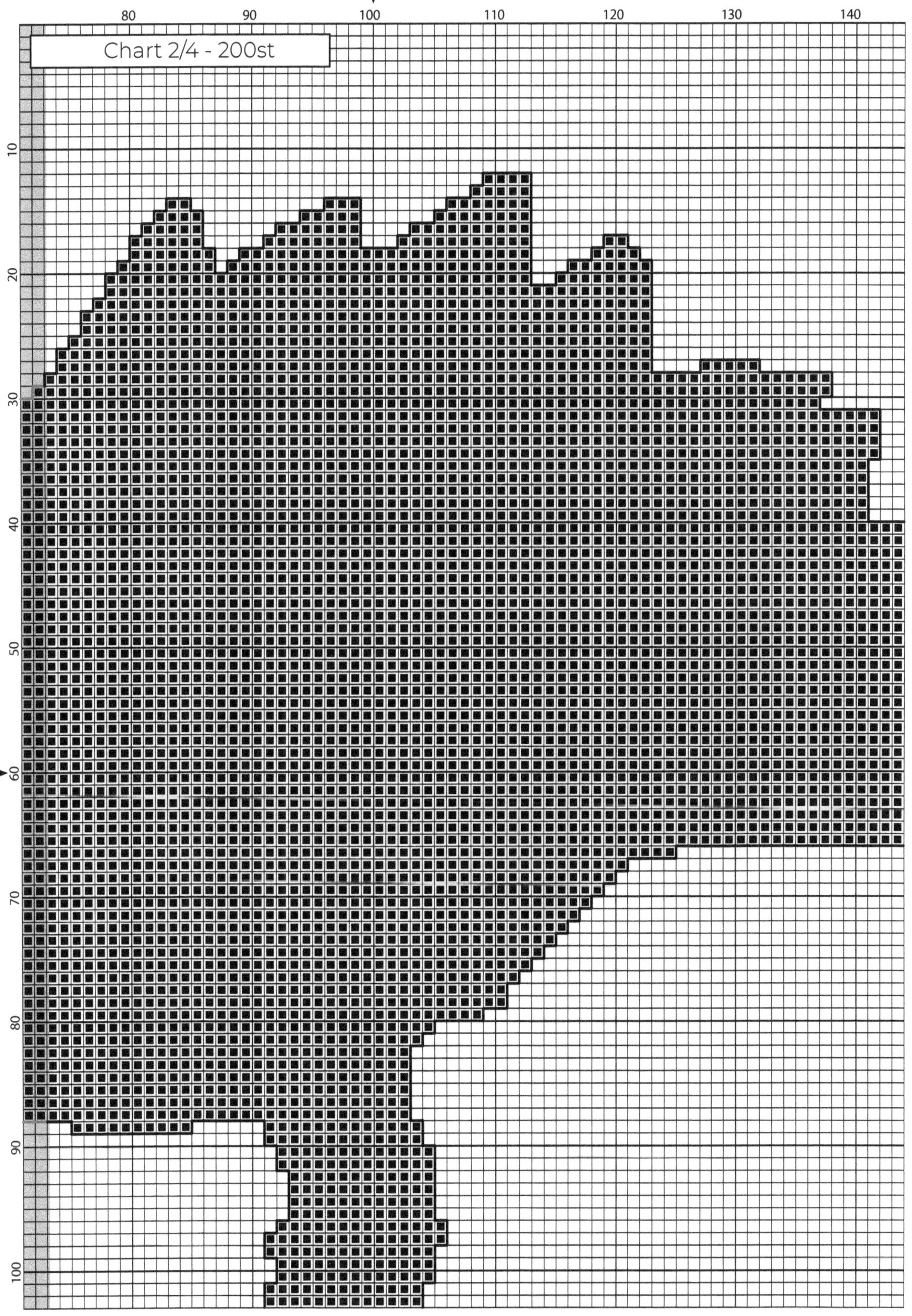

Chart 2/4 - 200st

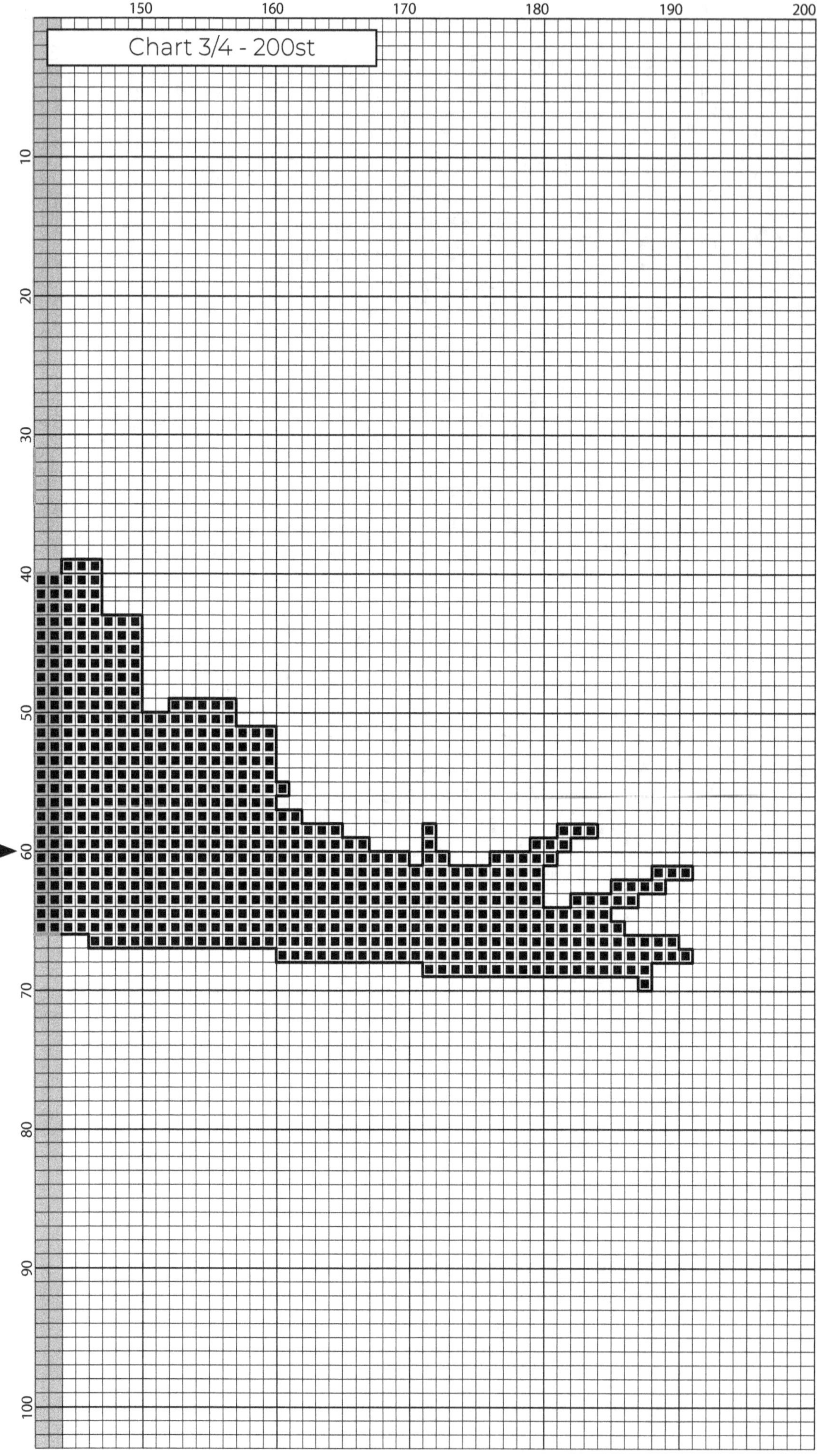

Chart 3/4 - 200st

Continued from page 30

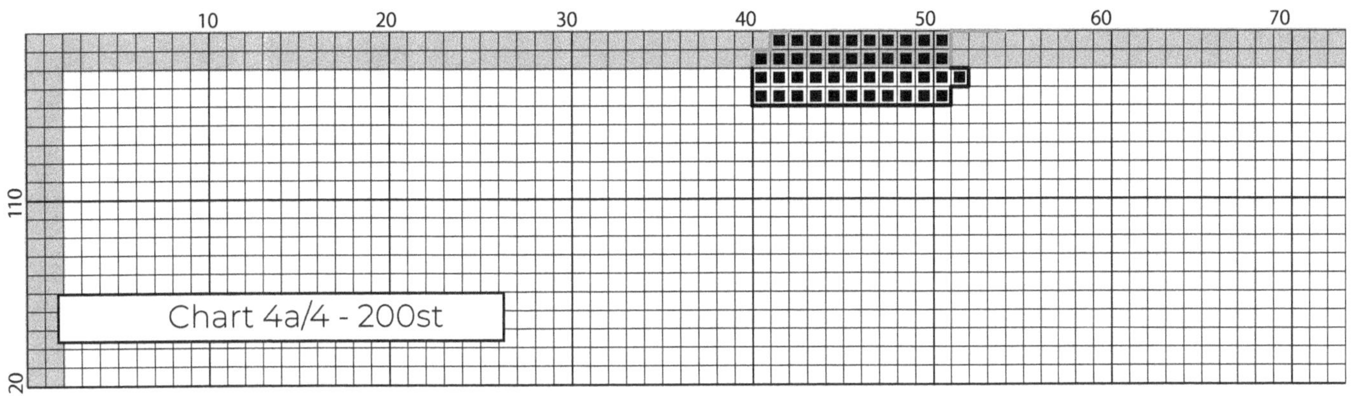

Continued from page 31

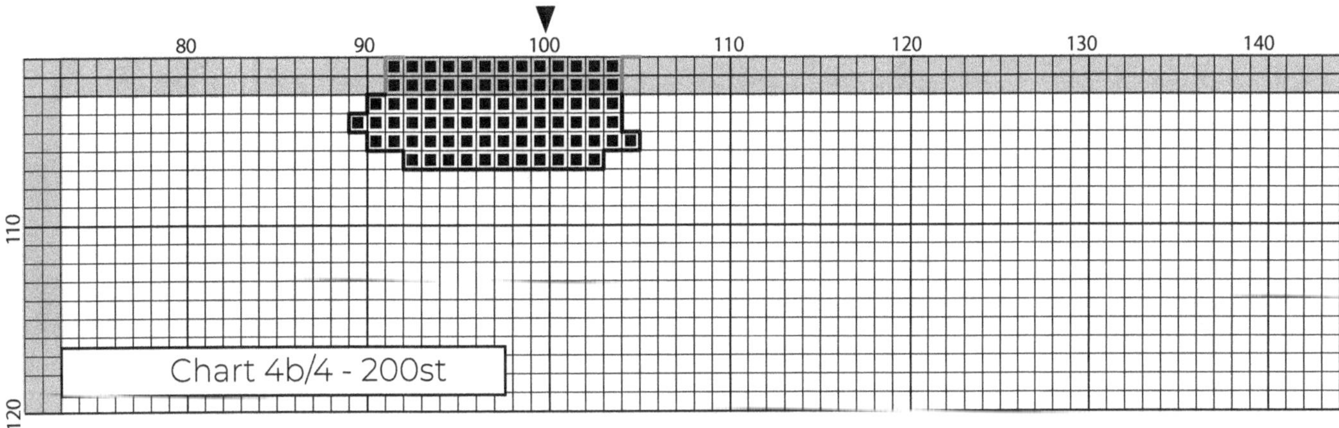

Styracosaurus

Grid Size: 100W x 70H
Design Area: 6.57" x 4.43" (92 x 62 stitches)

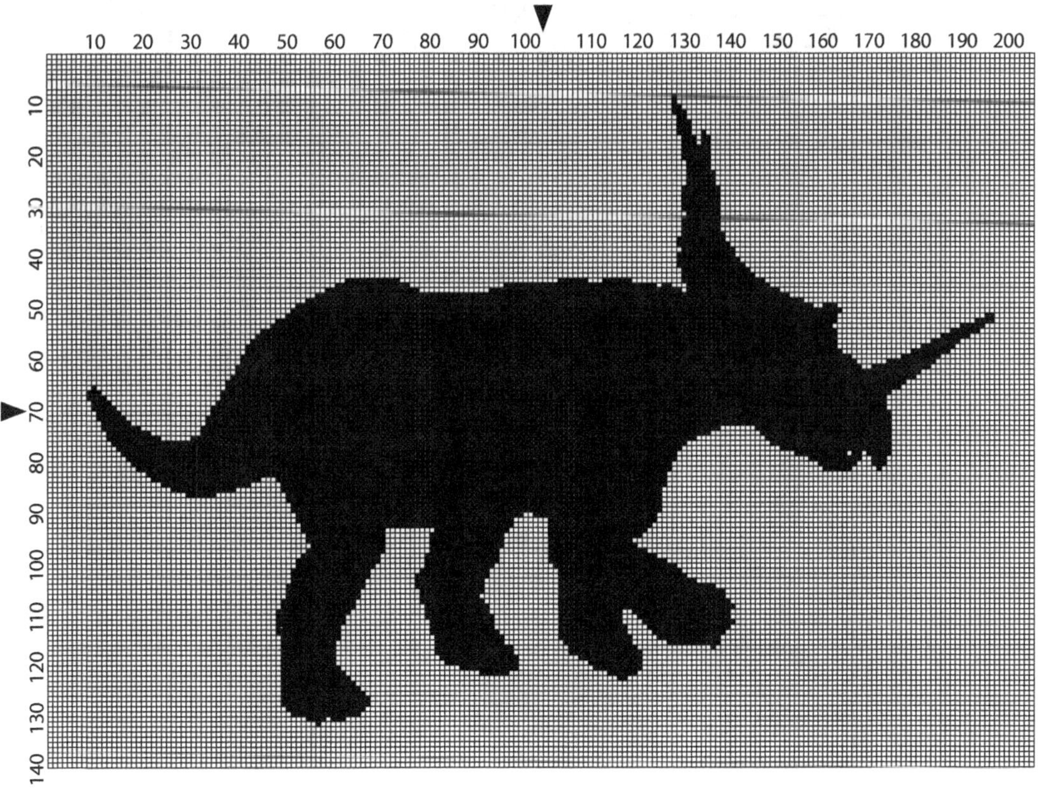

Grid Size: 200W x 140H
Design Area: 13.14" x 8.86" (184 x 124 stitches)

Chart 1/2 - 100st

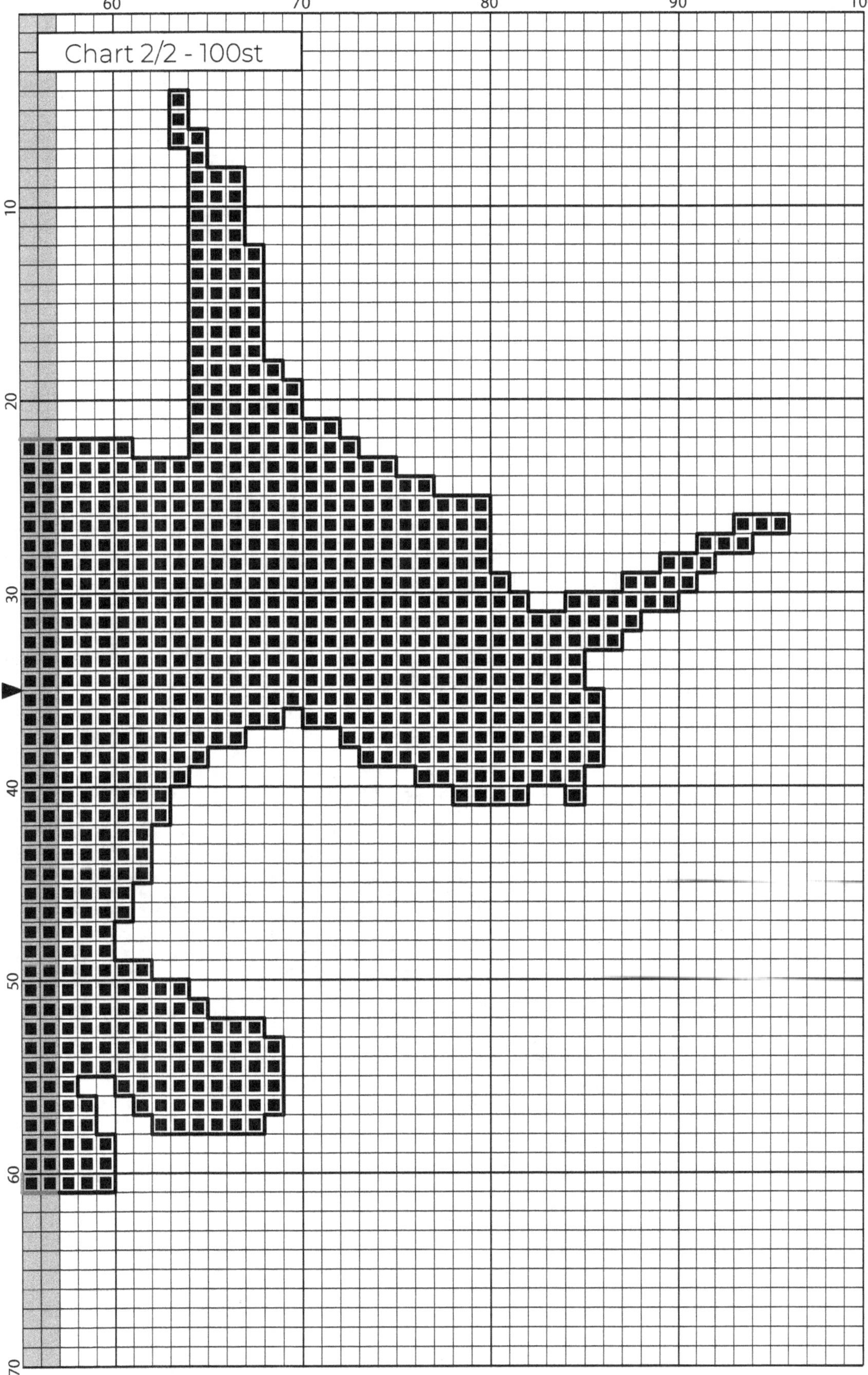

Chart 2/2 - 100st
60
70
80
90
100
10
20
30
40
50
60
70

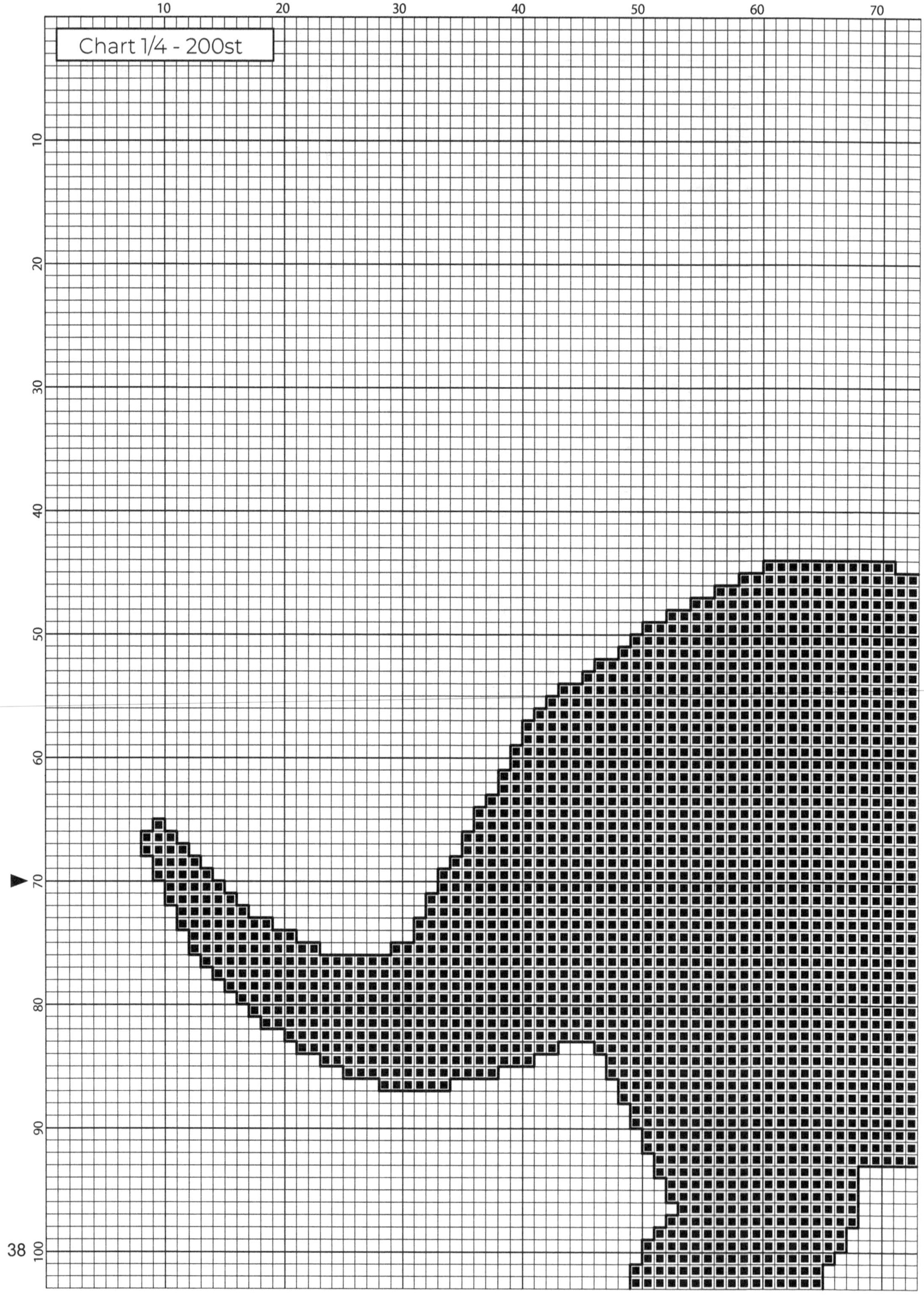

Chart 1/4 - 200st

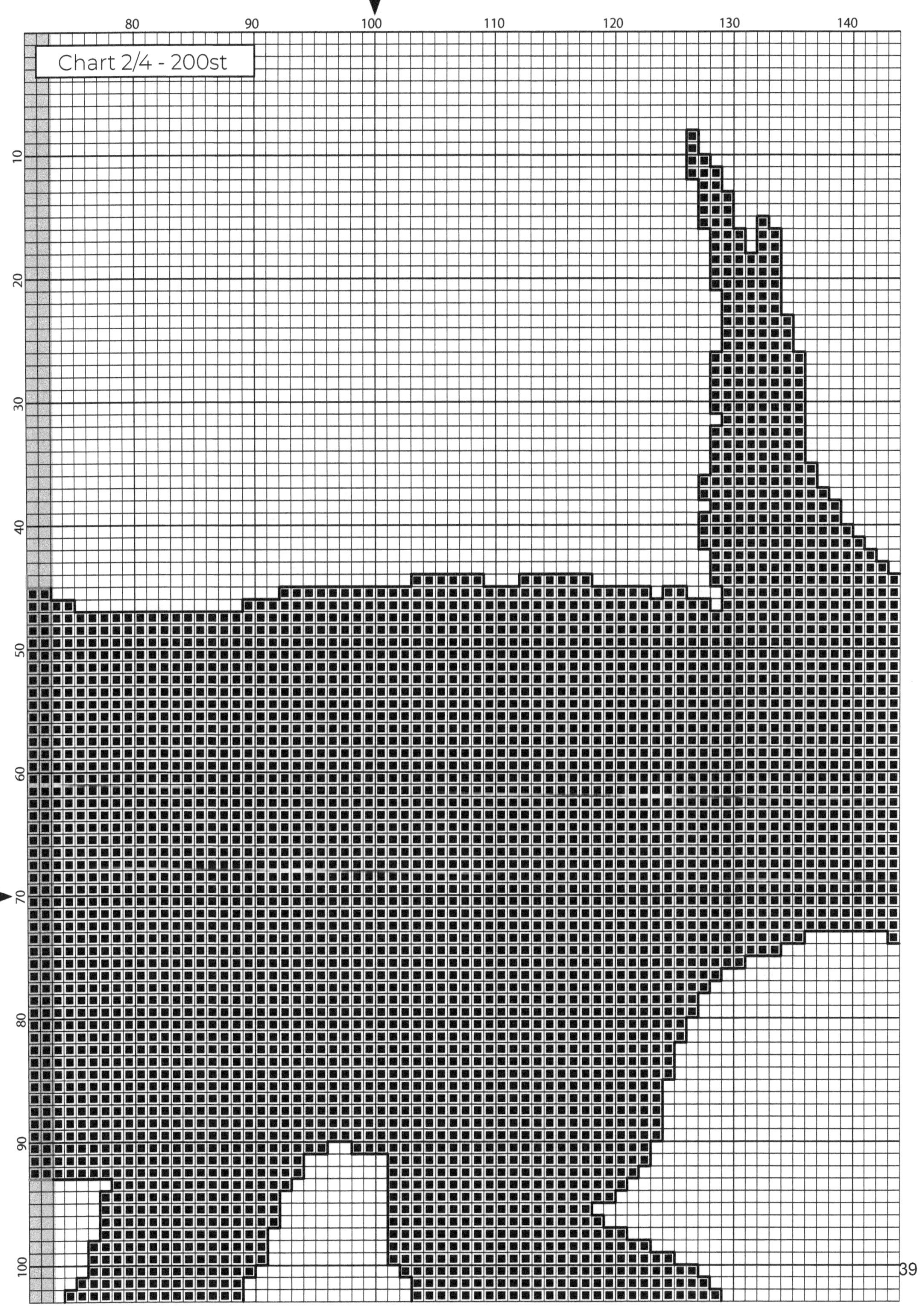Chart 2/4 - 200st
39

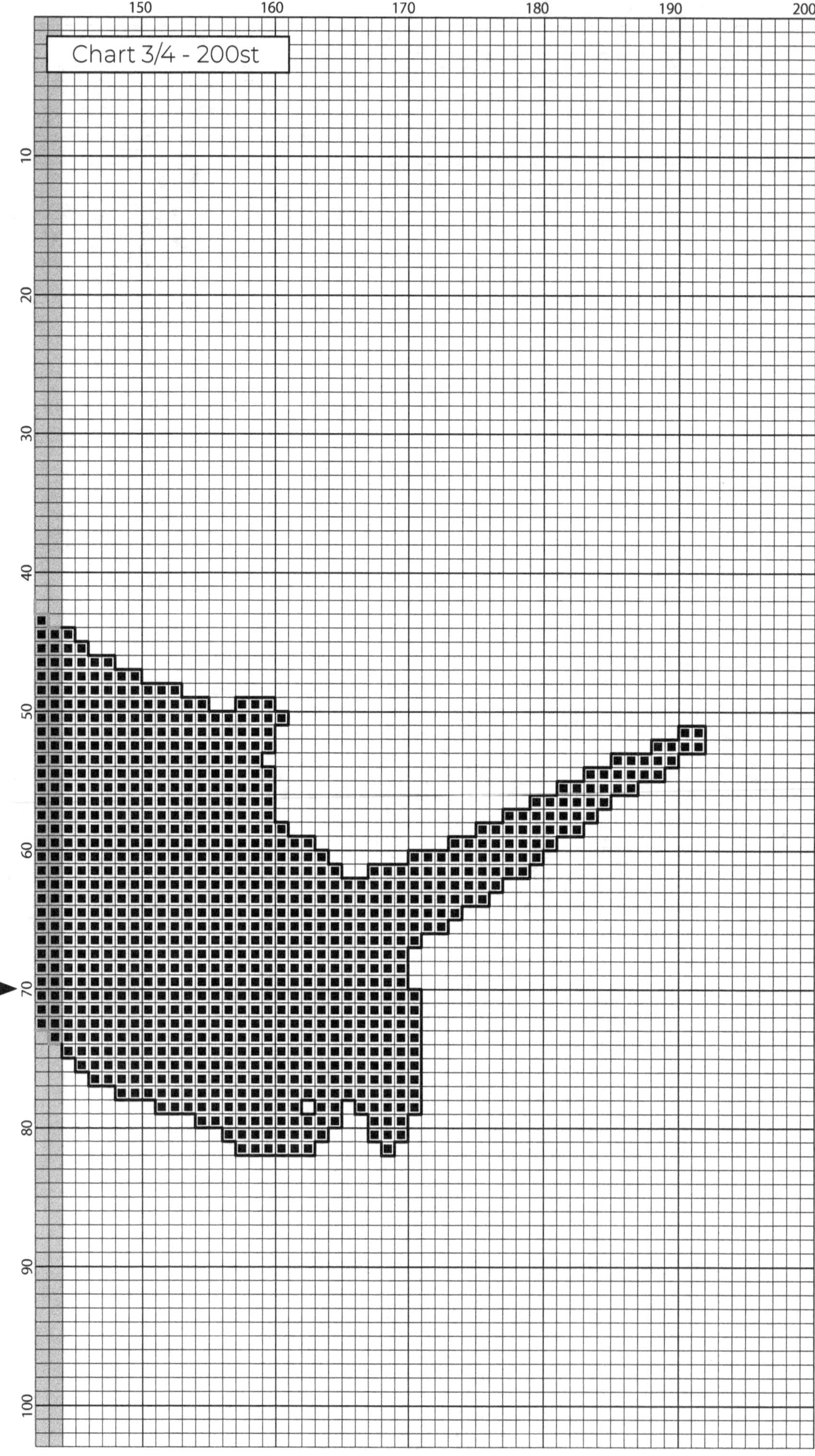

Chart 3/4 - 200st

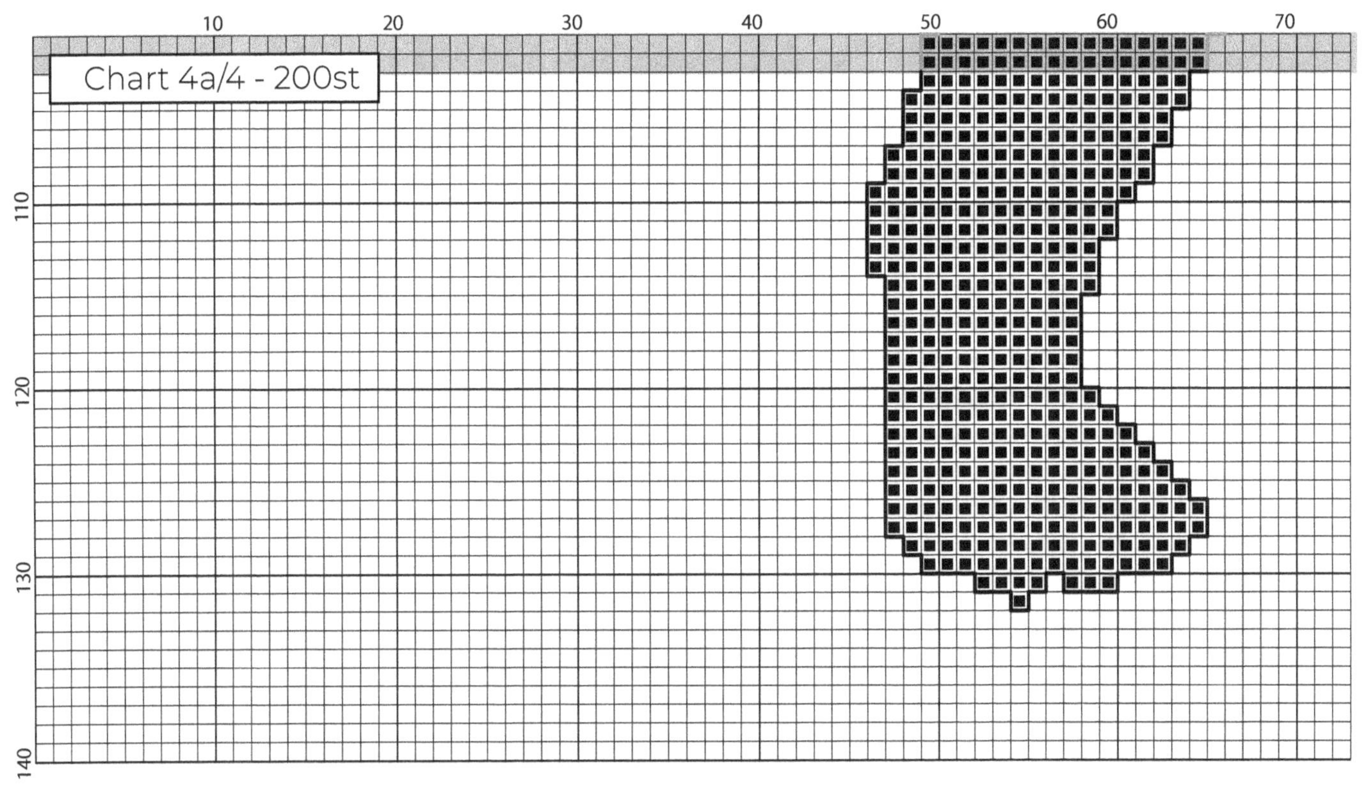

Chart 4a/4 - 200st

Continued from page 39

Chart 4b/4 - 200st

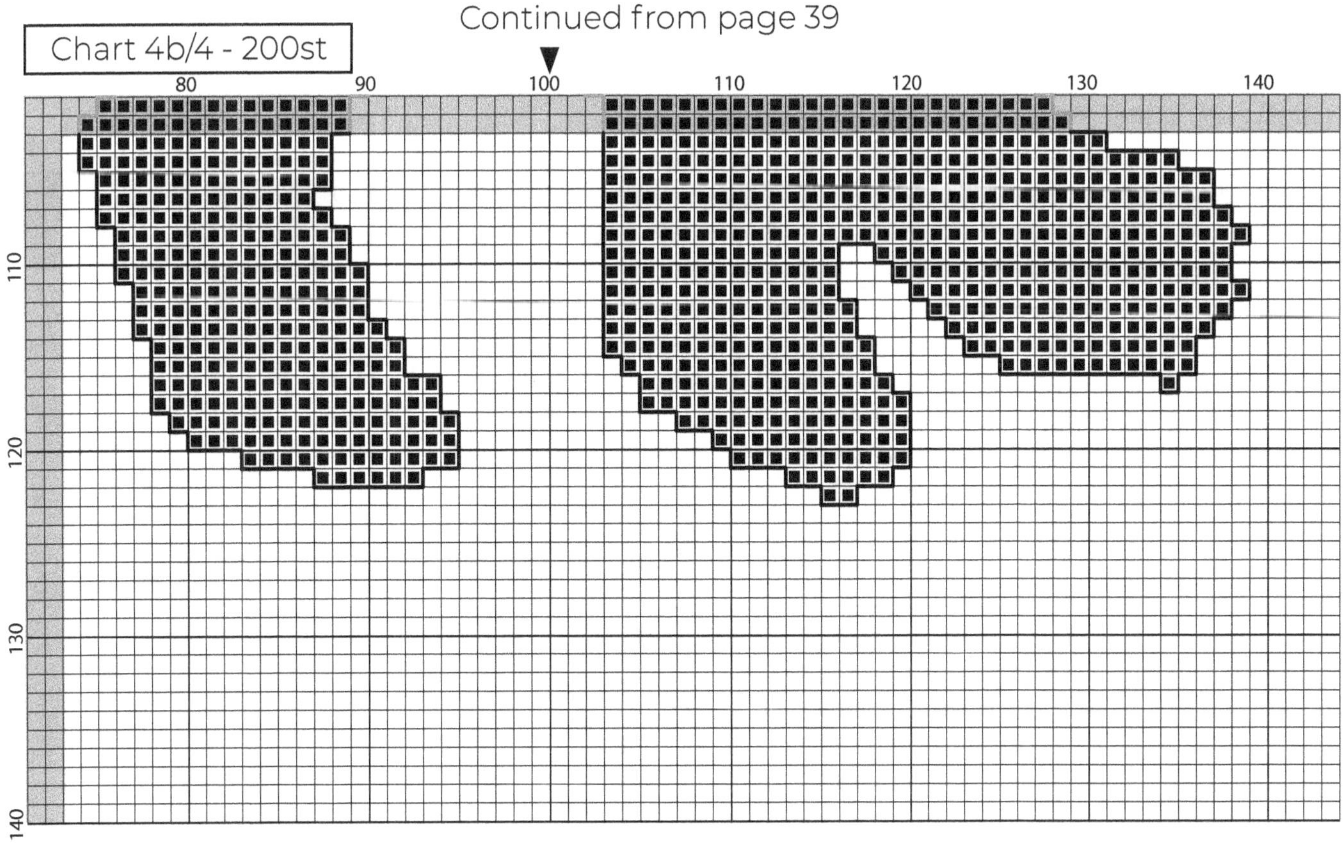

Triceratops

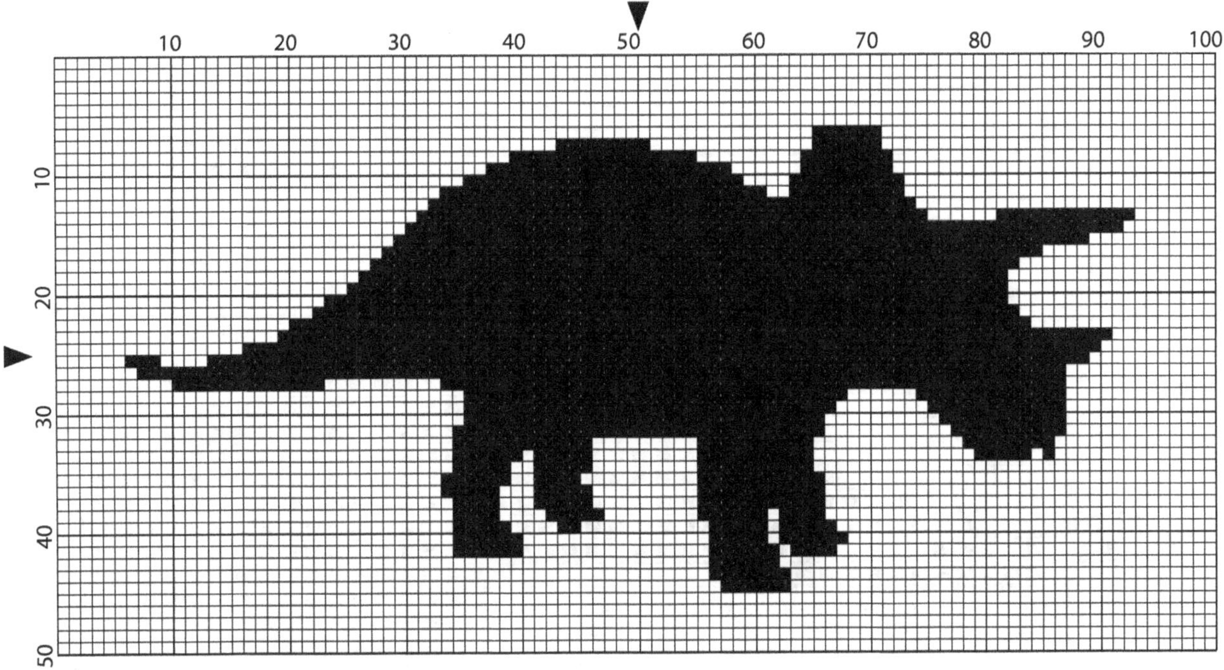

Grid Size: 100W x 50H
Design Area: 6.21" x 2.79" (87 x 39 stitches)

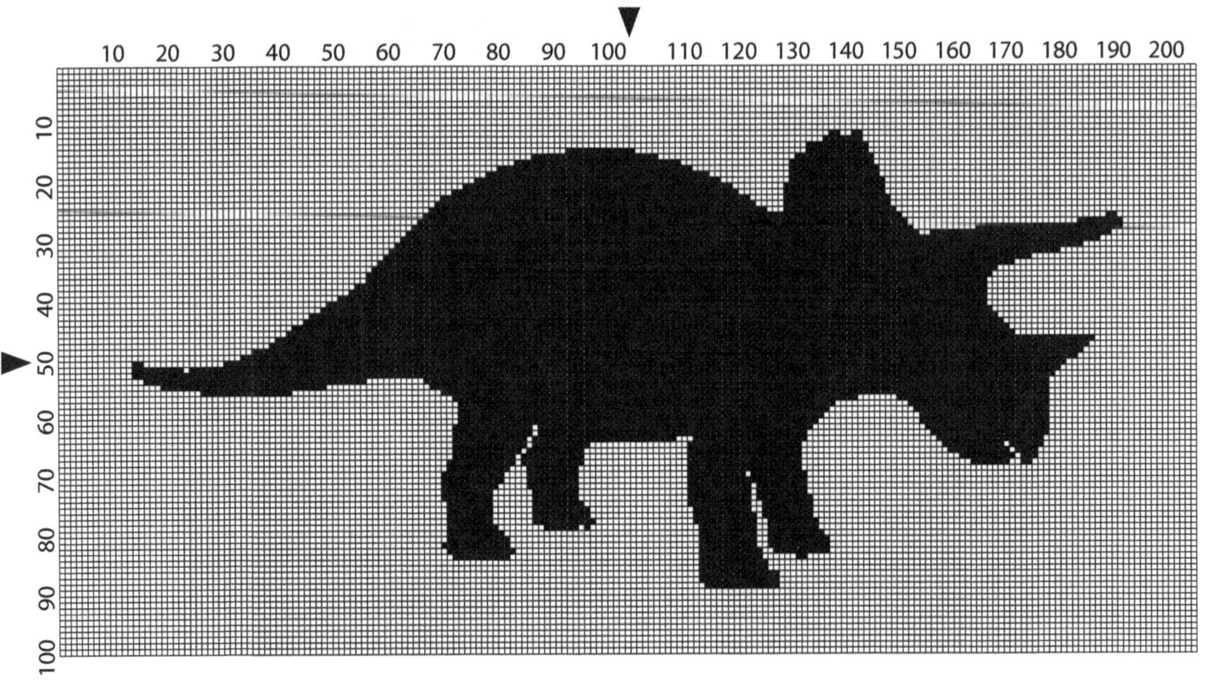

Grid Size: 200W x 100H
Design Area: 12.43" x 5.57" (174 x 78 stitches)

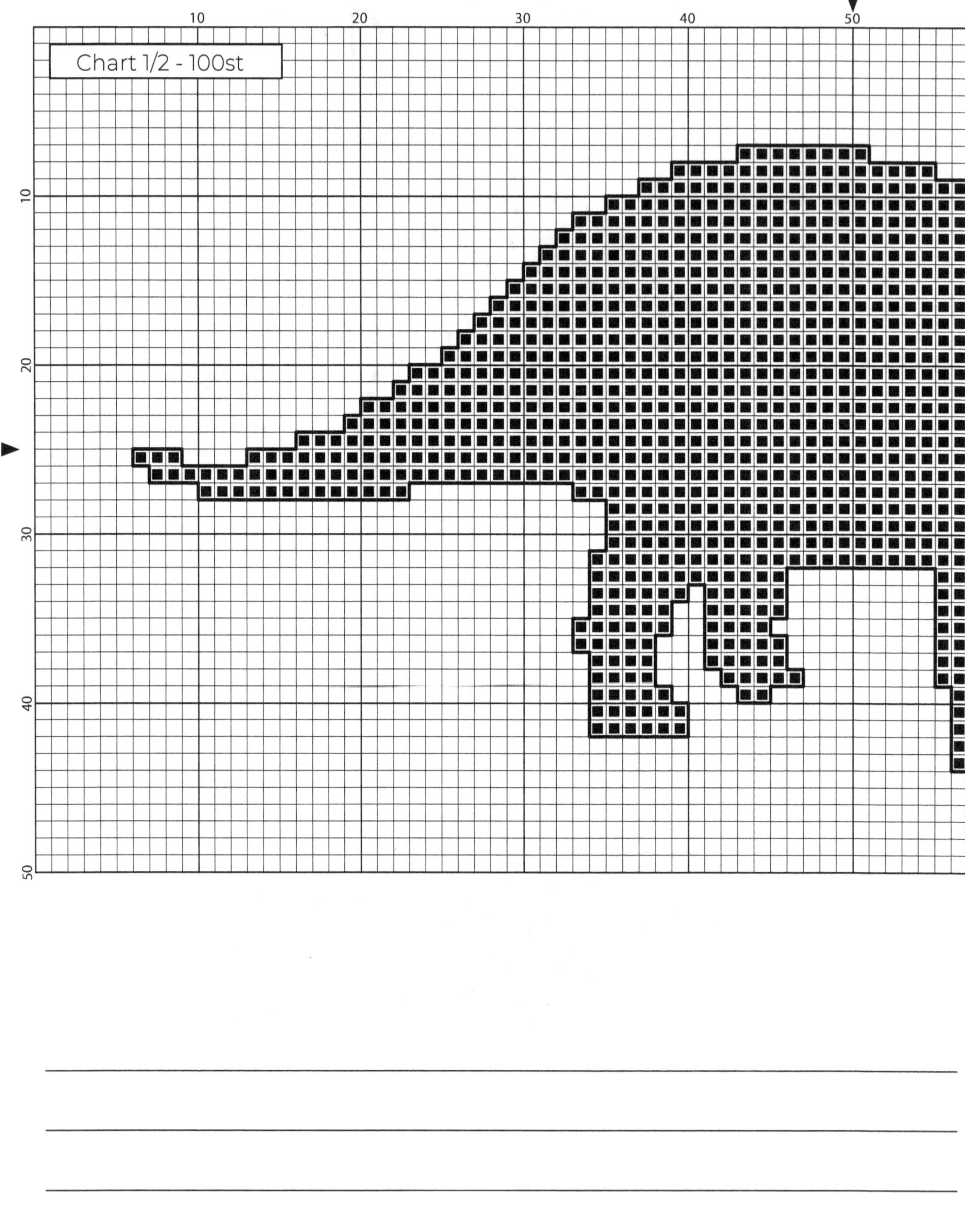

Chart 1/2 - 100st

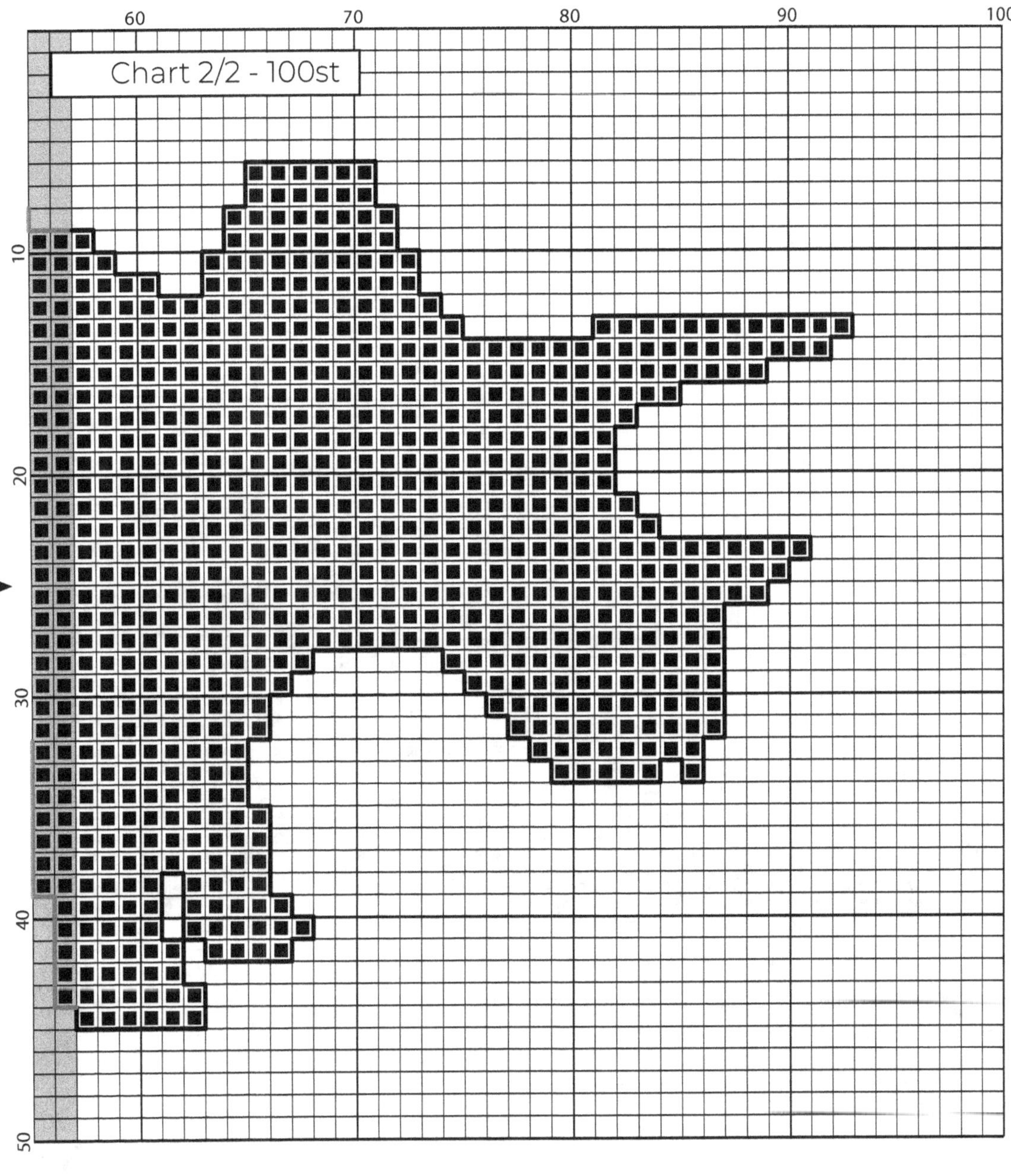

Chart 2/2 - 100st

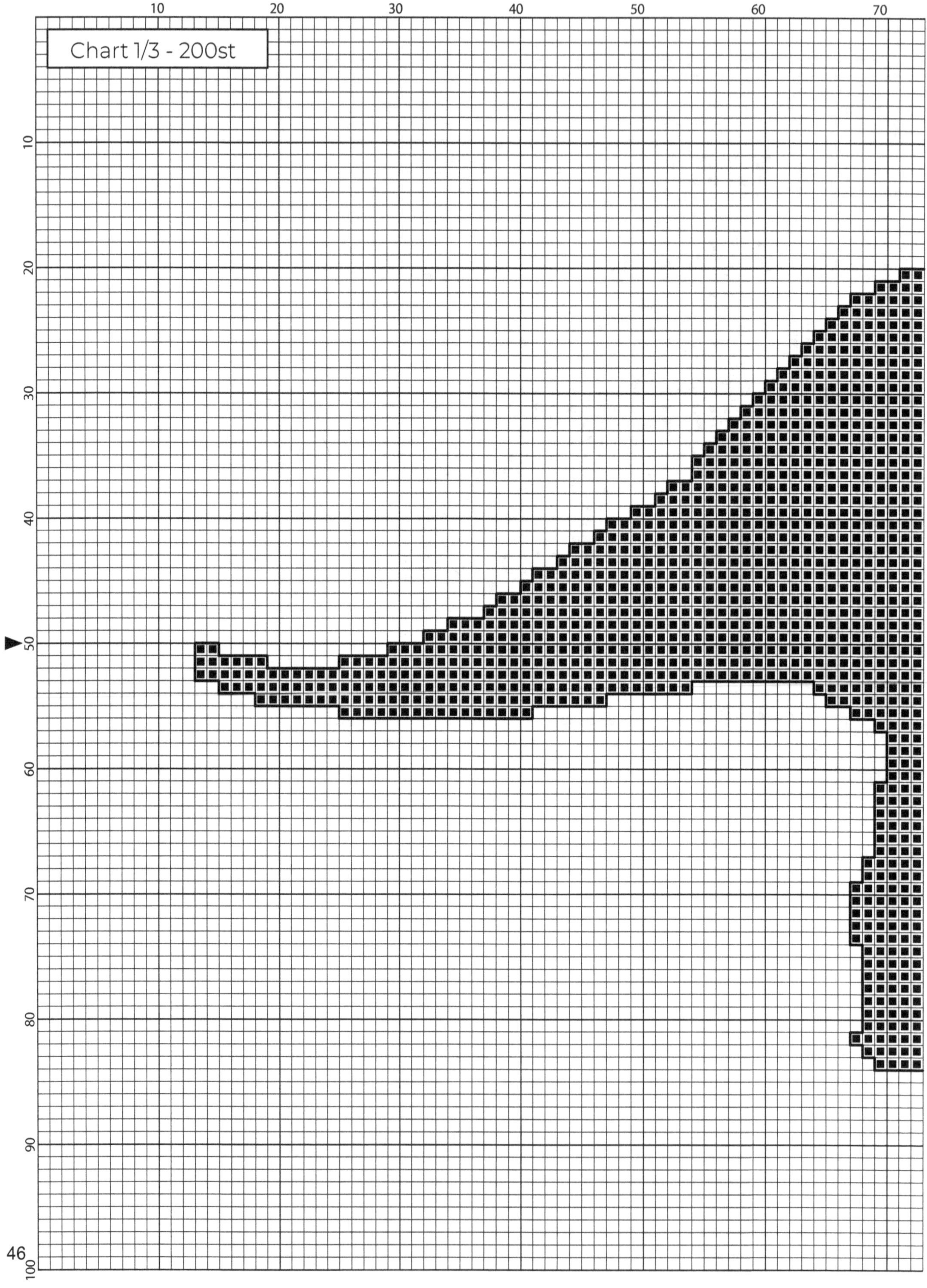

Chart 1/3 - 200st

Chart 2/3 - 200st
47

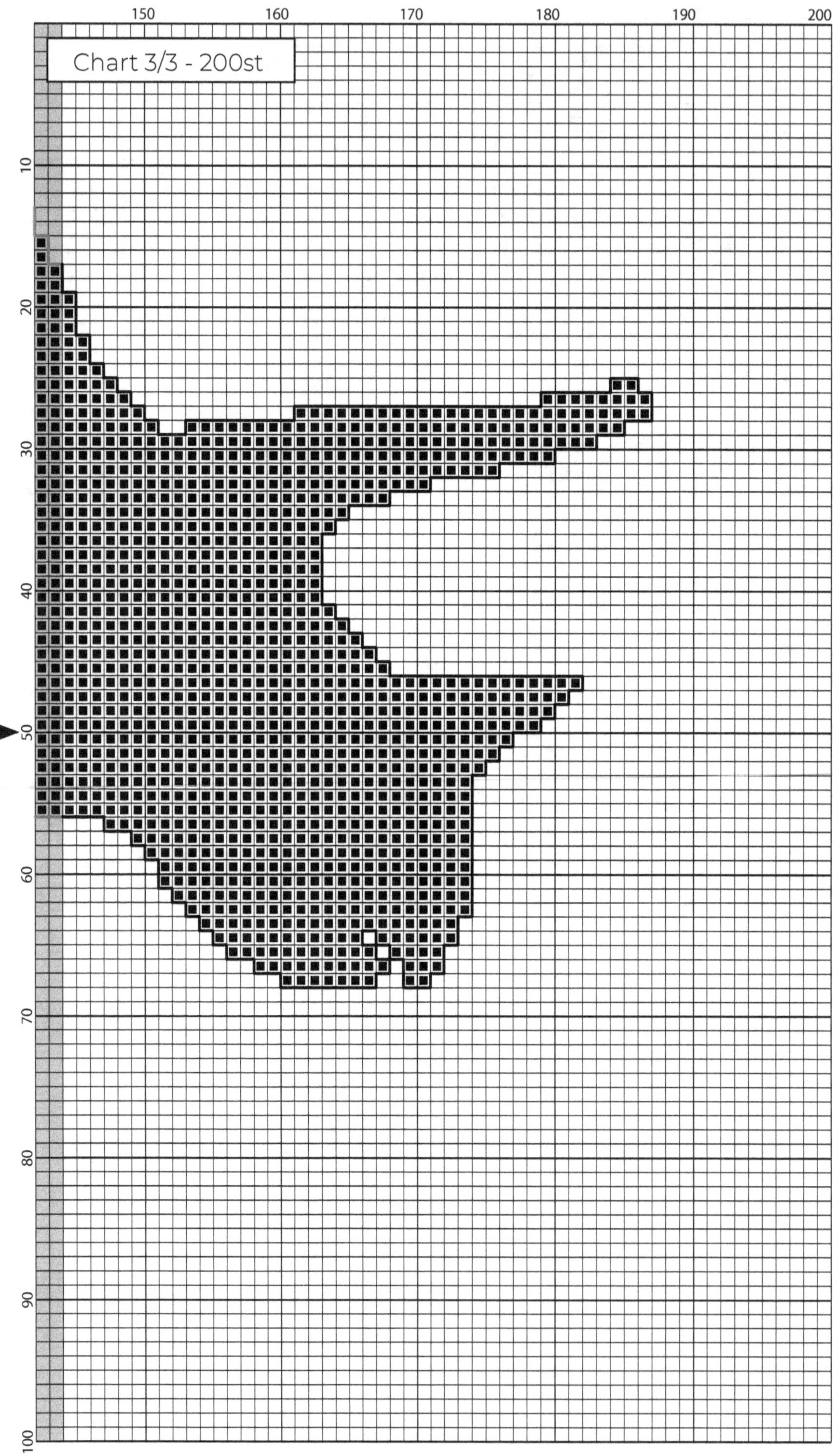

T-Rex

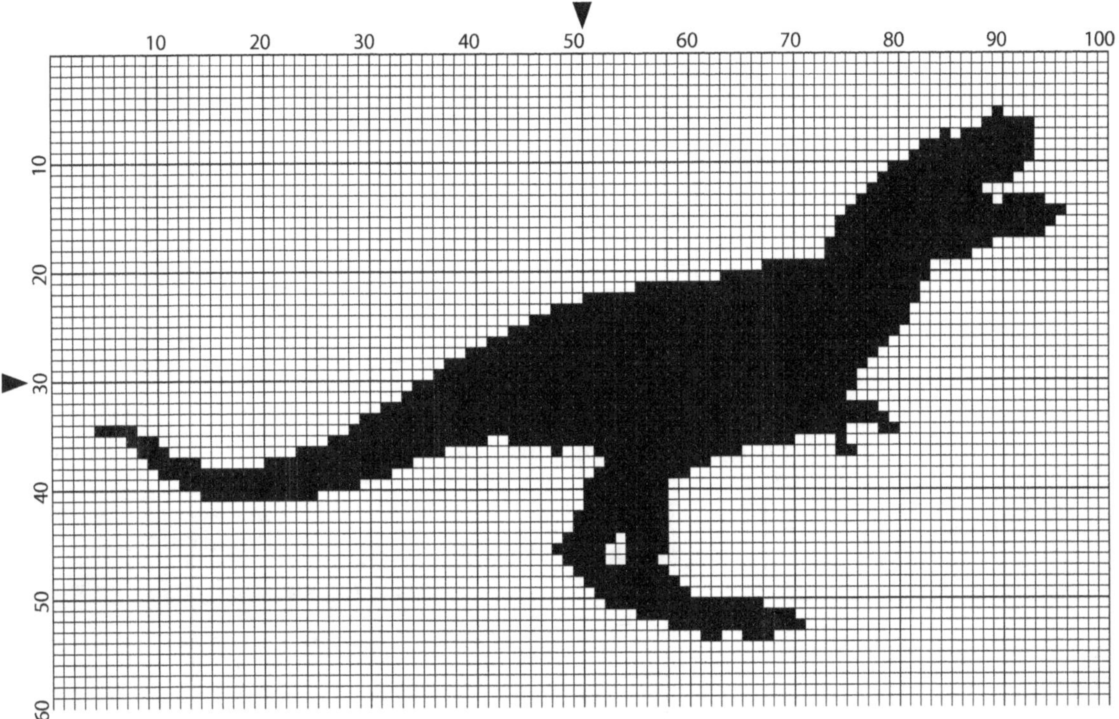

Grid Size: 100W x 60H
Design Area: 6.57" x 3.50" (92 x 49 stitches)

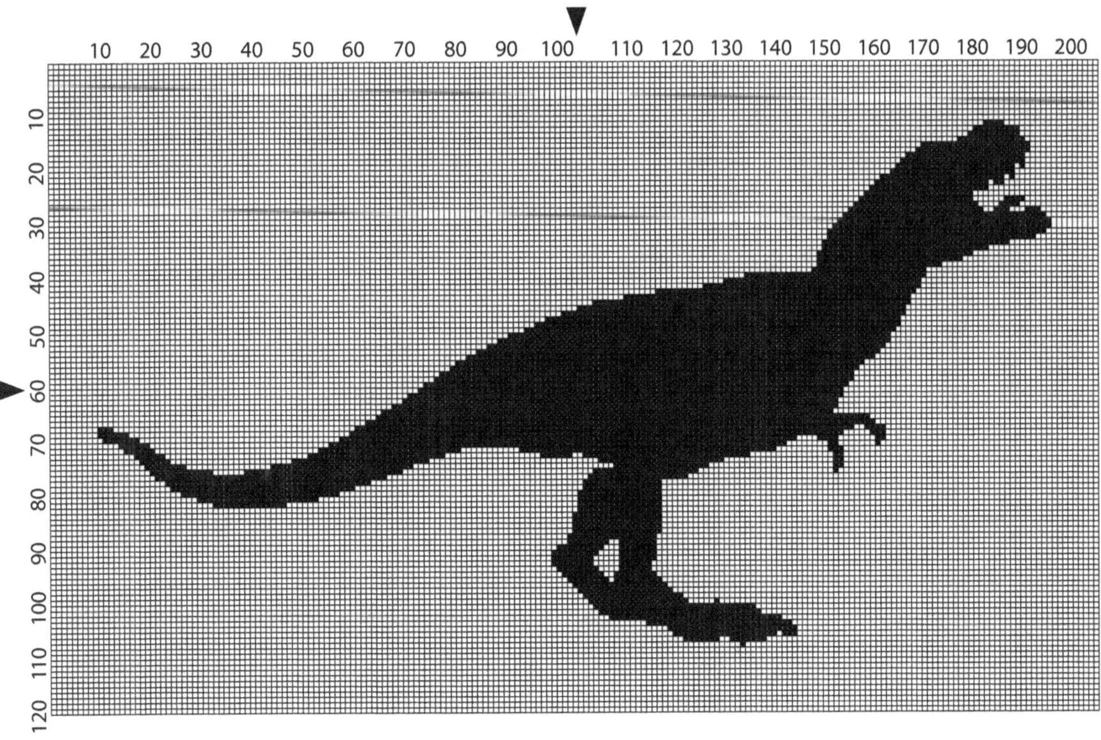

Grid Size: 200W x 120H
Design Area: 13.00" x 6.93" (182 x 97 stitches)

10
20
30
40
50
Chart 1/2 - 100st
10
20
30
40
50
60

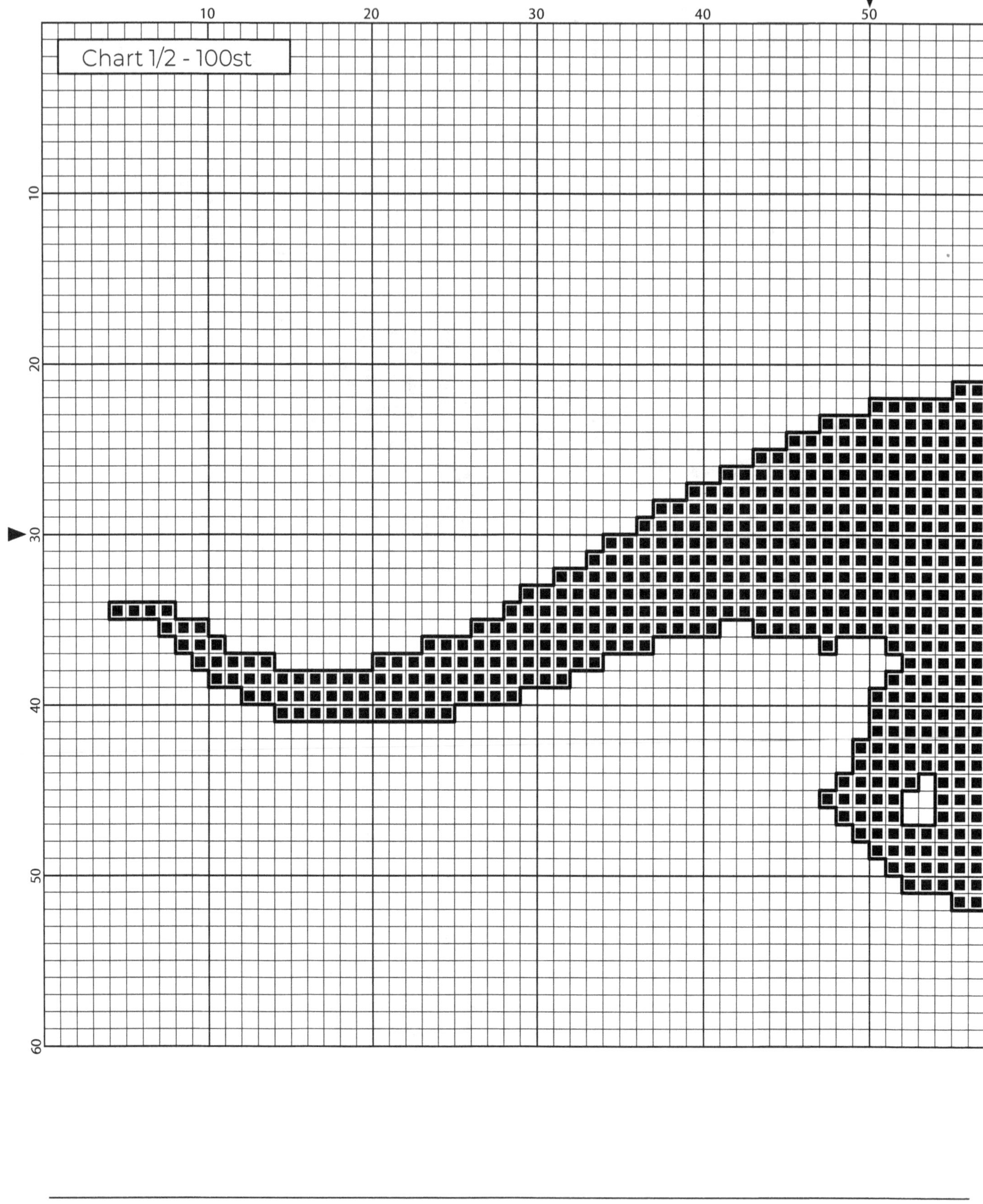

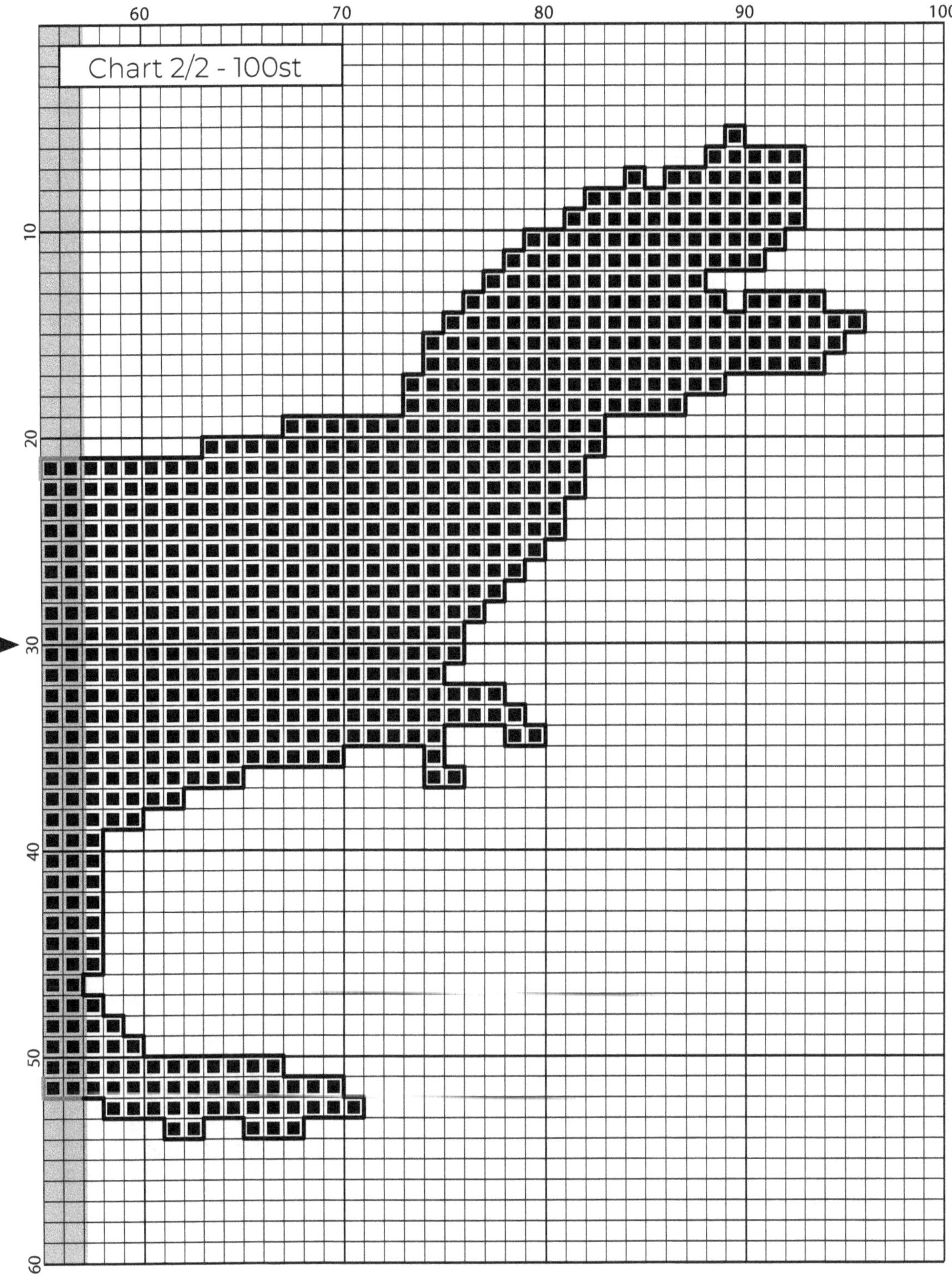

Chart 2/2 - 100st

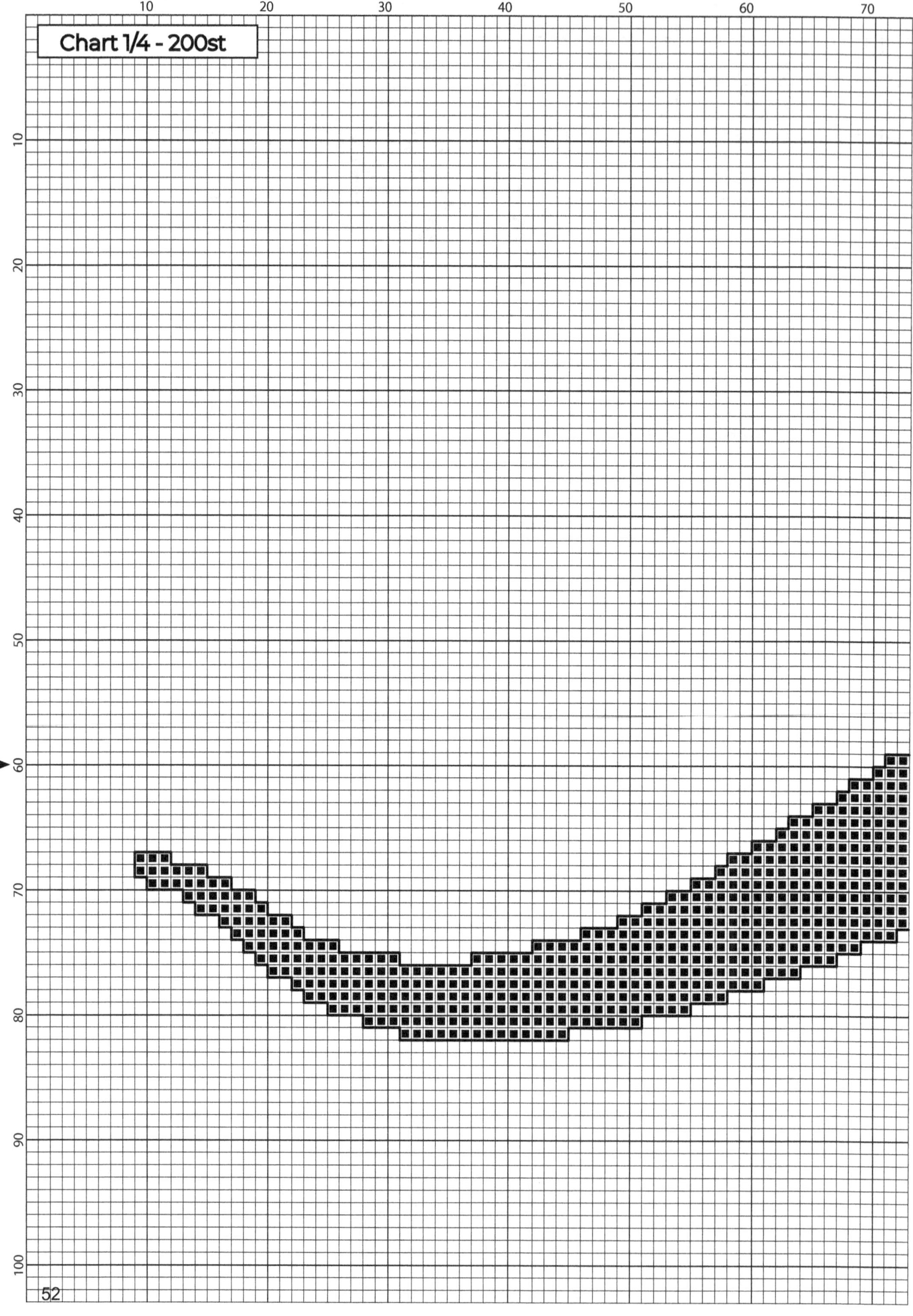

Chart 1/4 - 200st
52

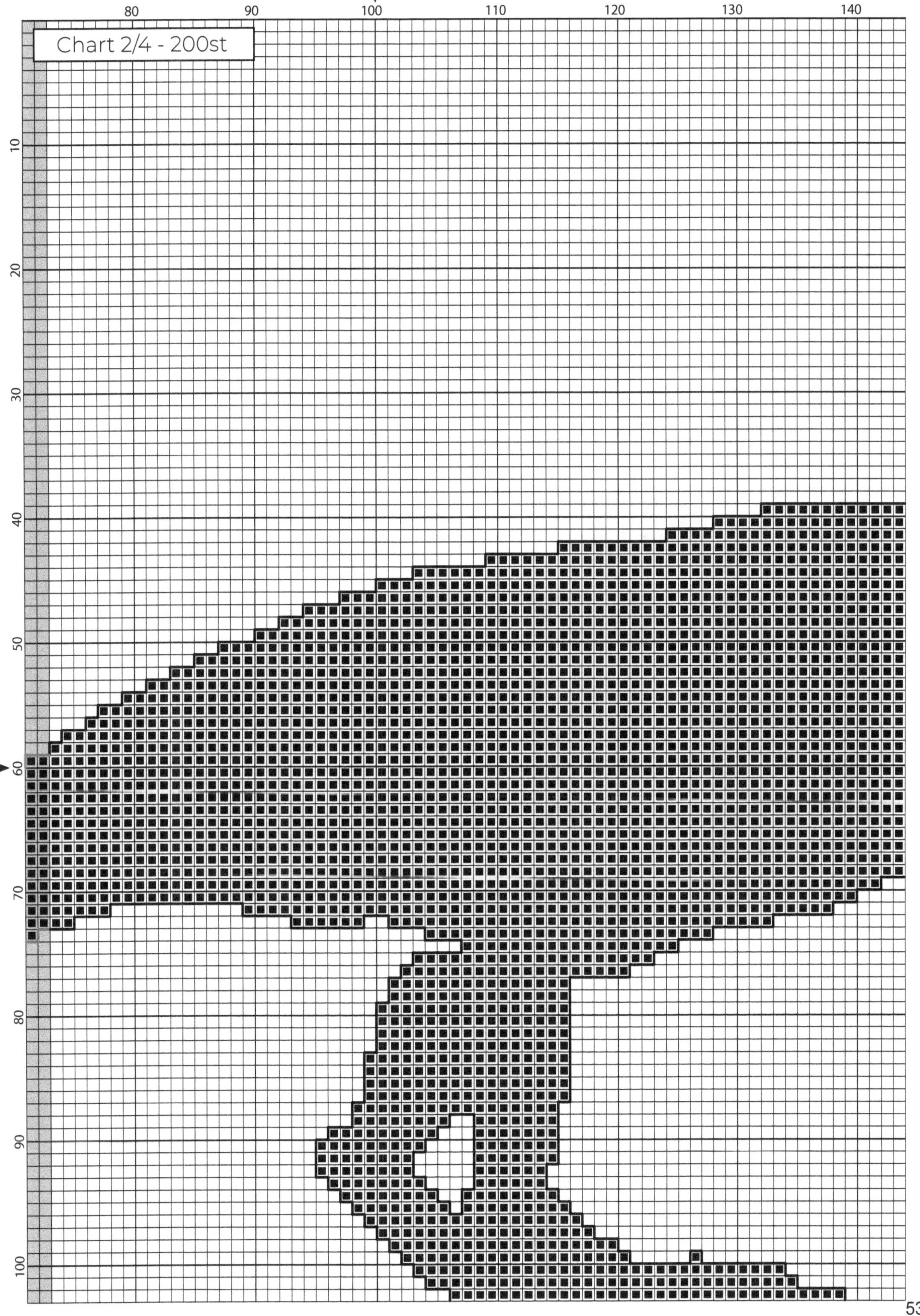

Chart 2/4 - 200st

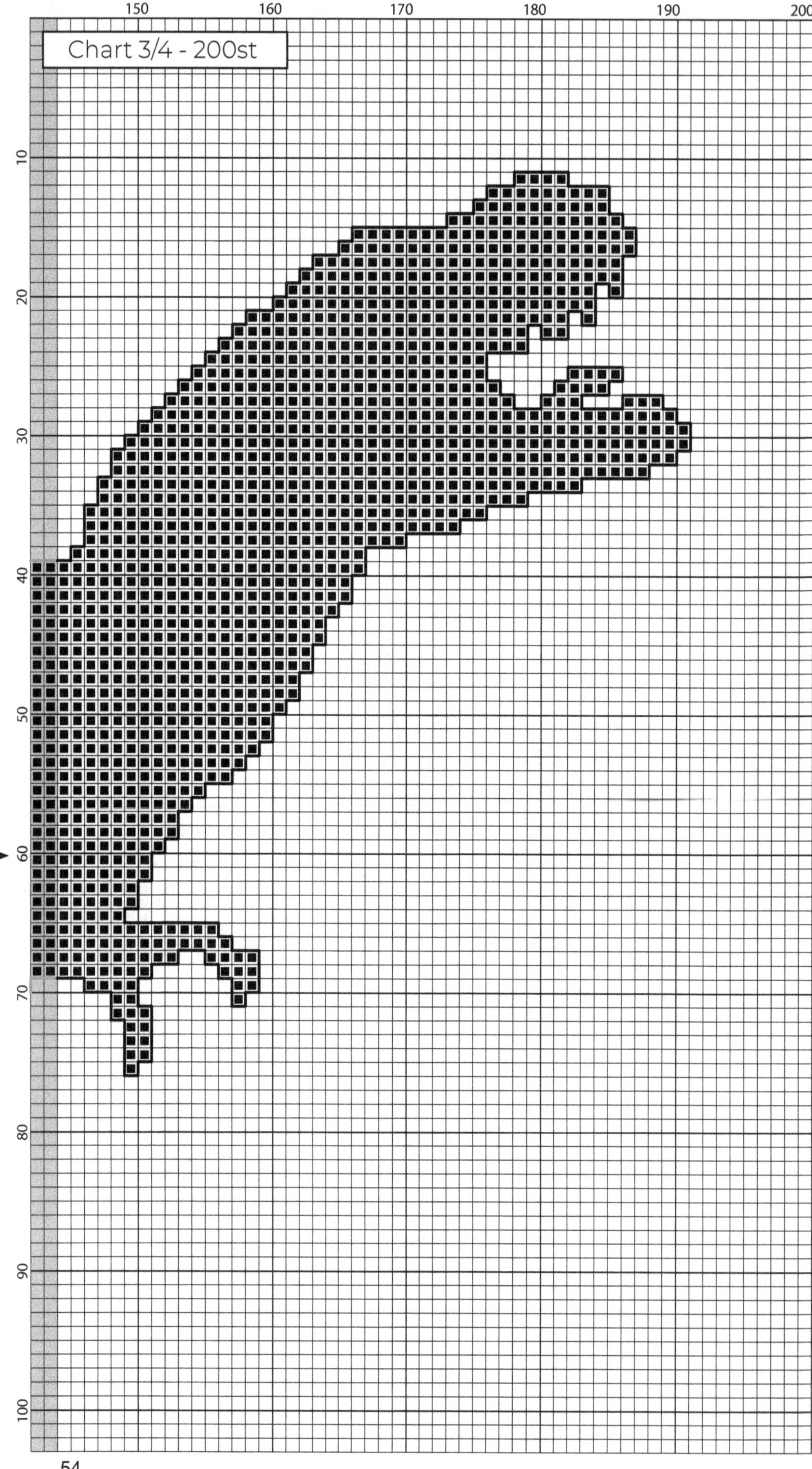

150
160
170
180
190
200
10
20
30
40
50
60
70
80
90
100
Chart 3/4 - 200st
54

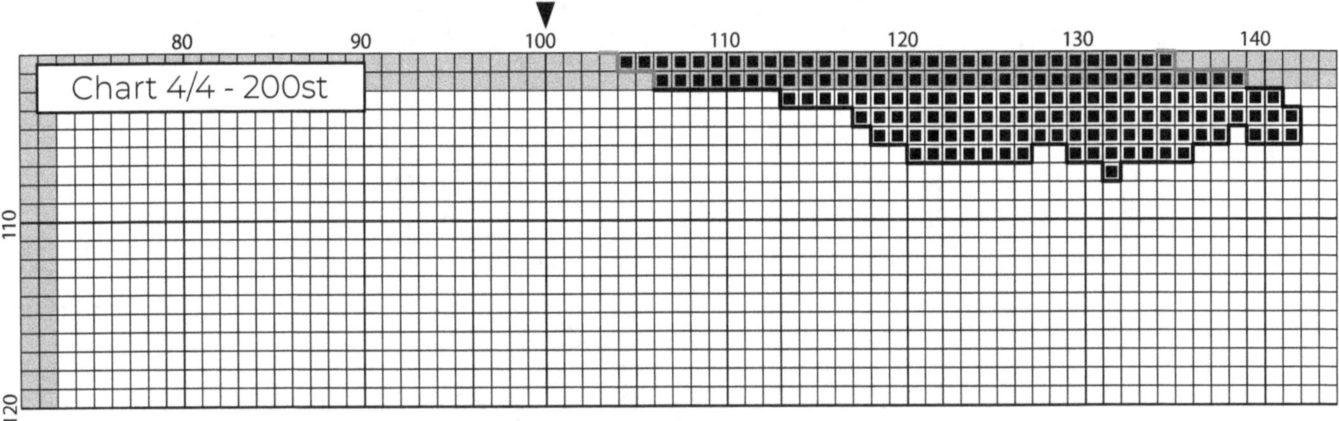
Chart 4/4 - 200st
80
90
100
110
120
130
140
110
120

ALLOSAURUS
APATOSAURUS
PTERANODON
SPINOSAURUS
STEGOSAURUS
STYRACOSAURUS
TRICERATOPS
T-REX

notes & sketches

notes & sketches

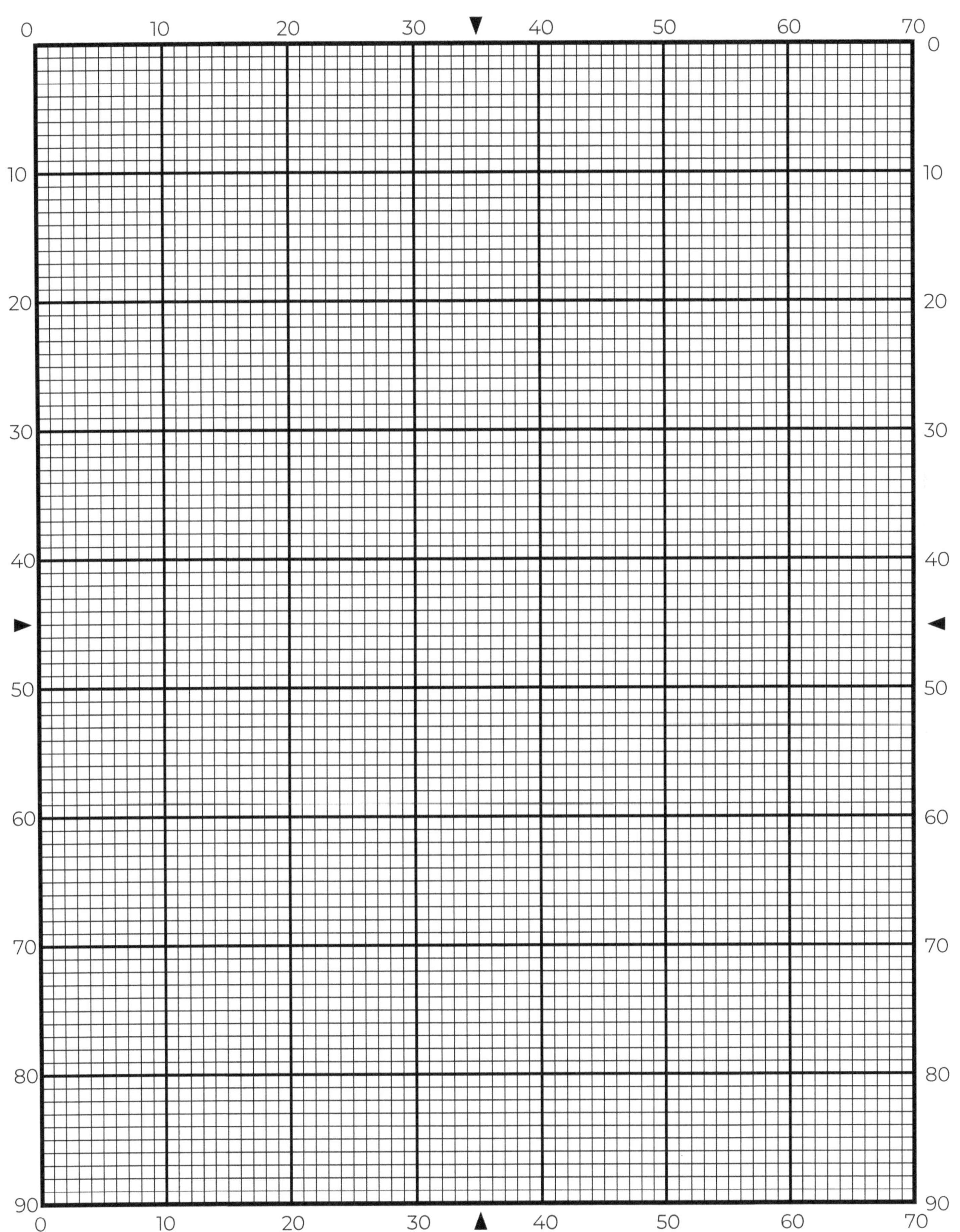

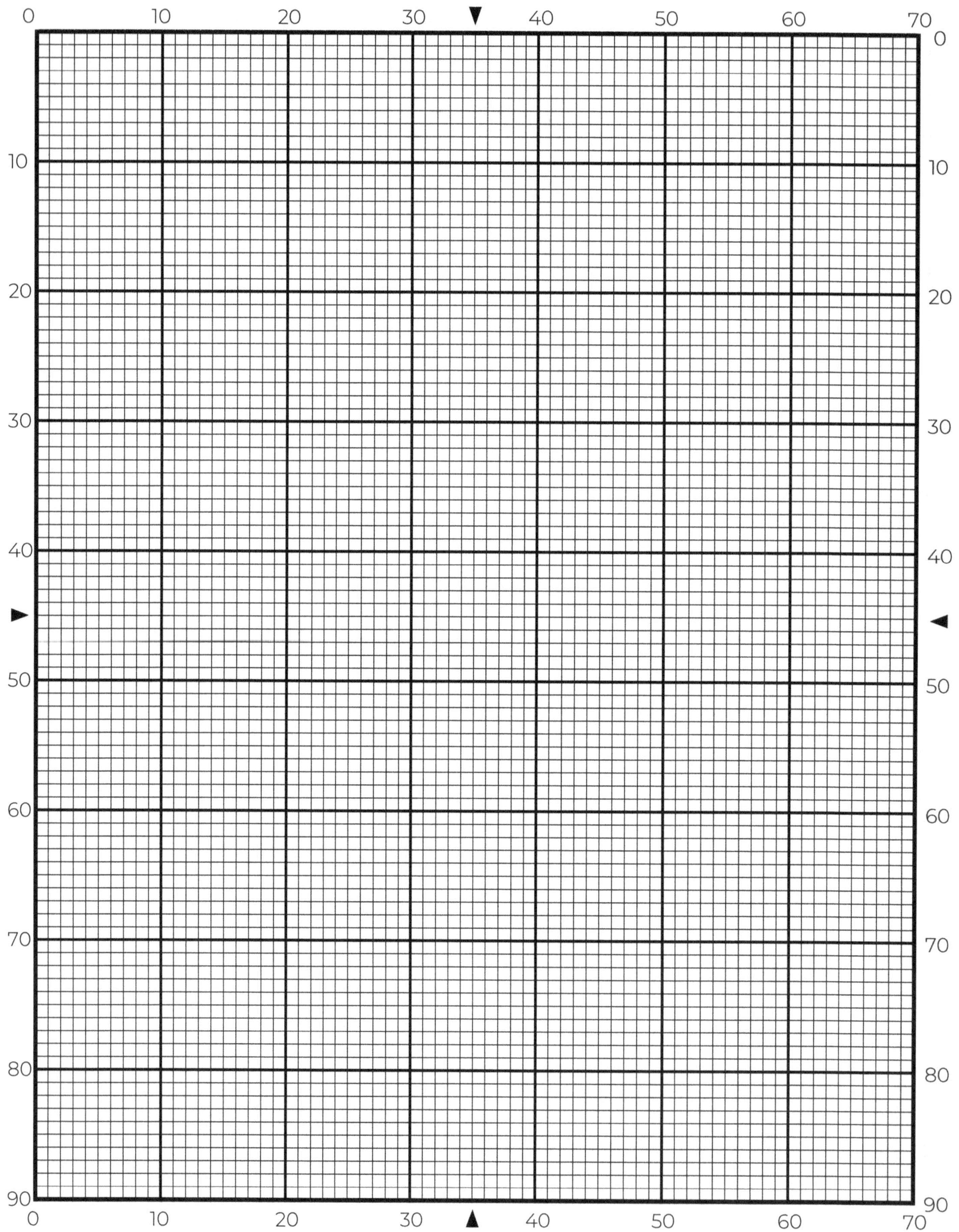

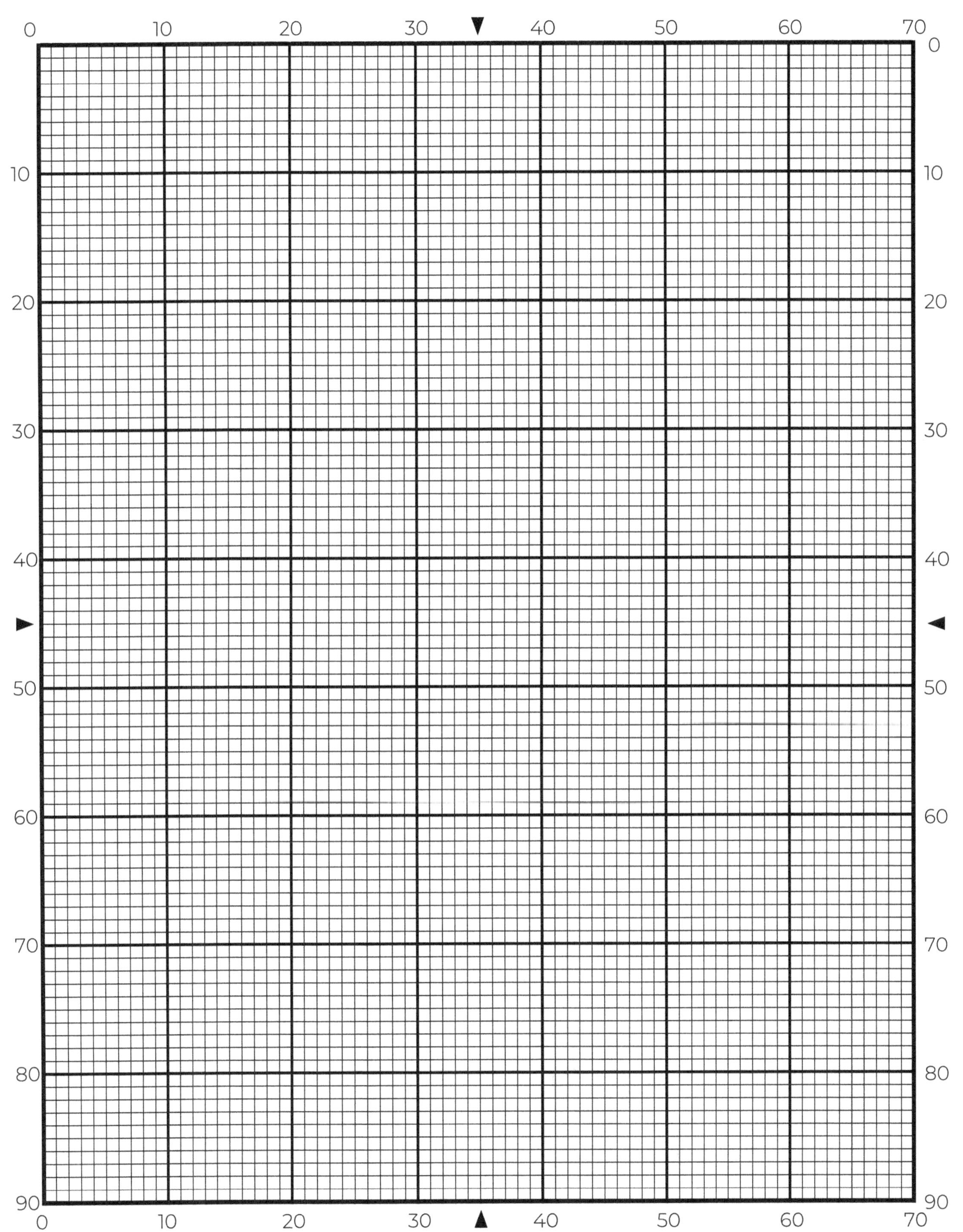

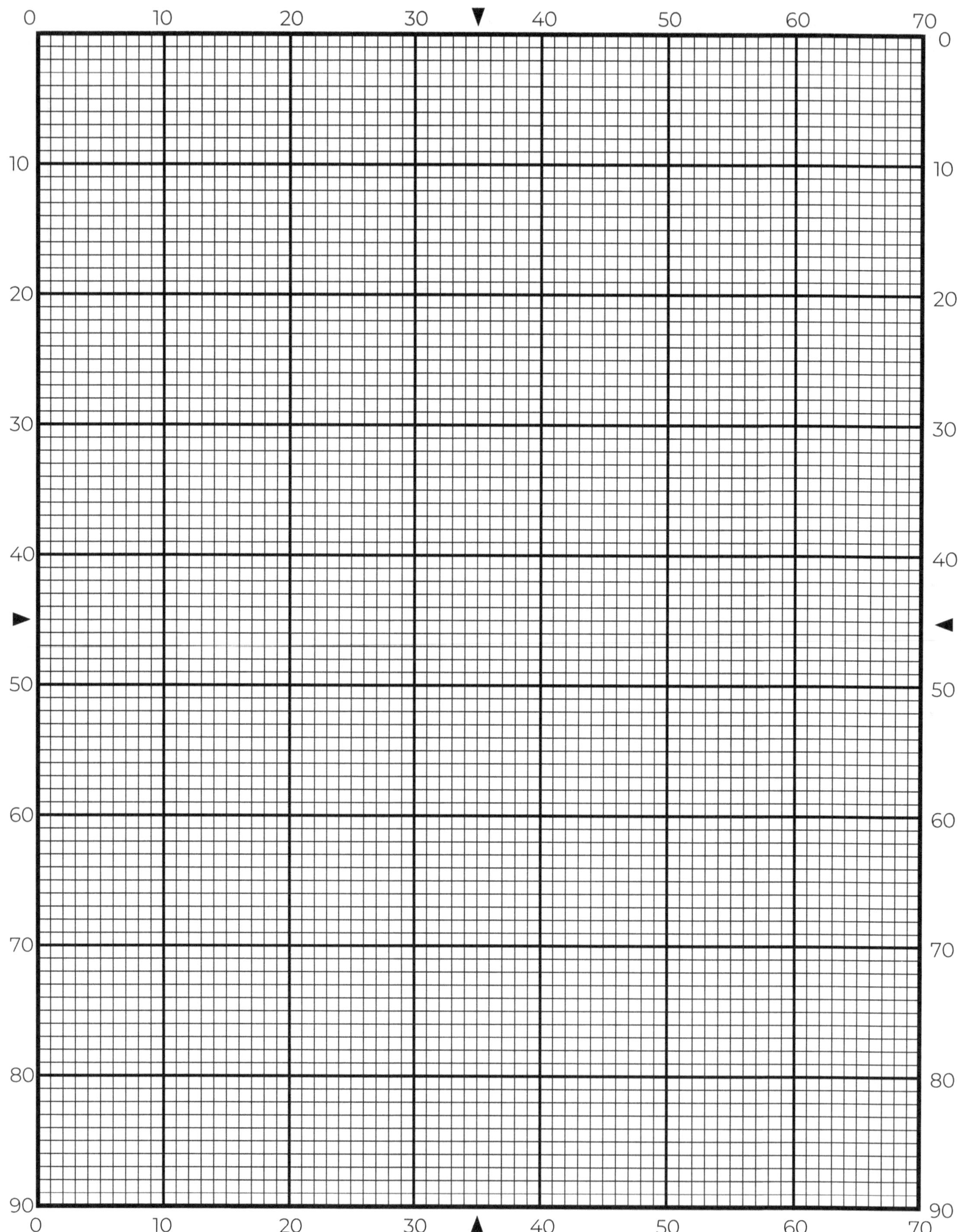

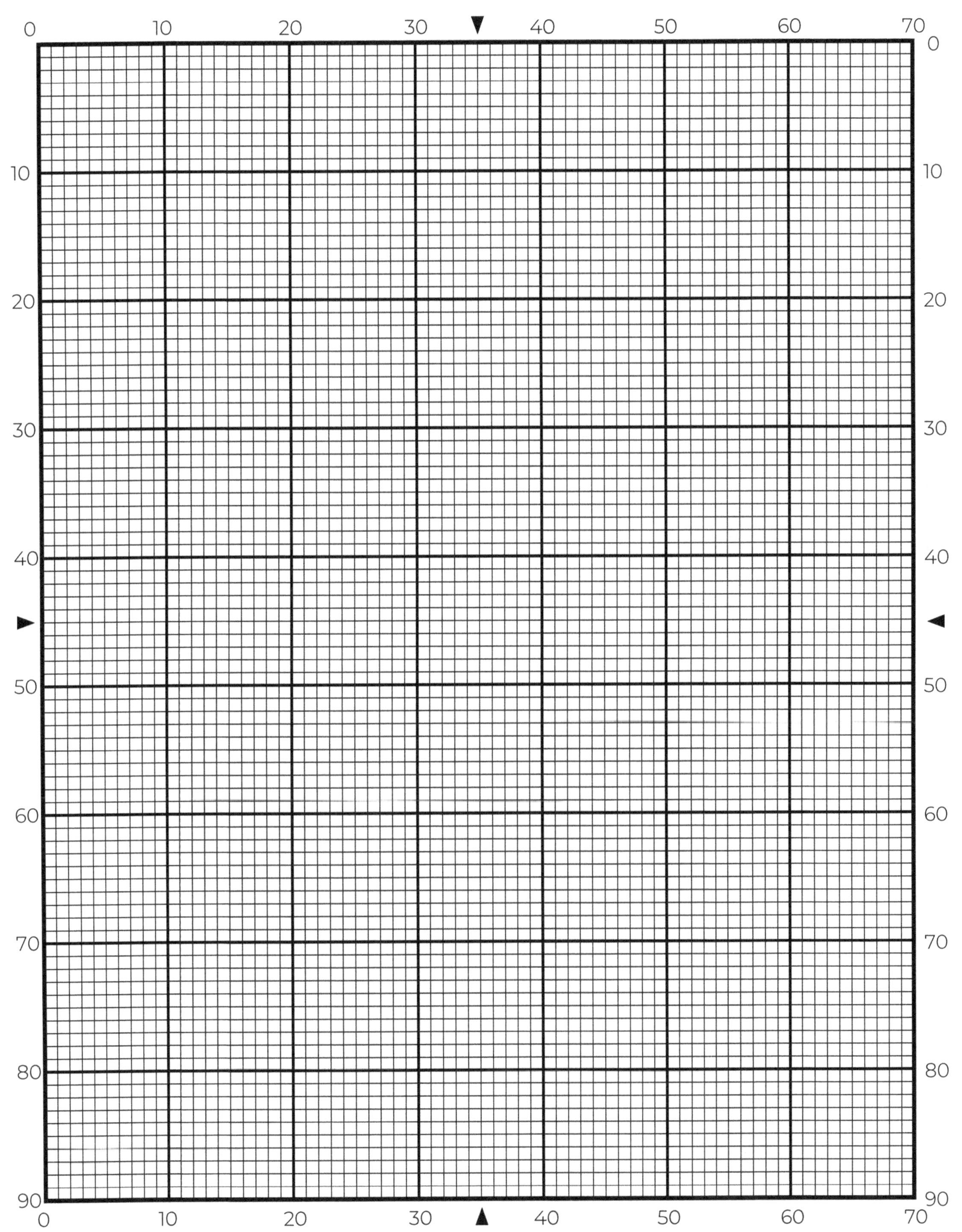

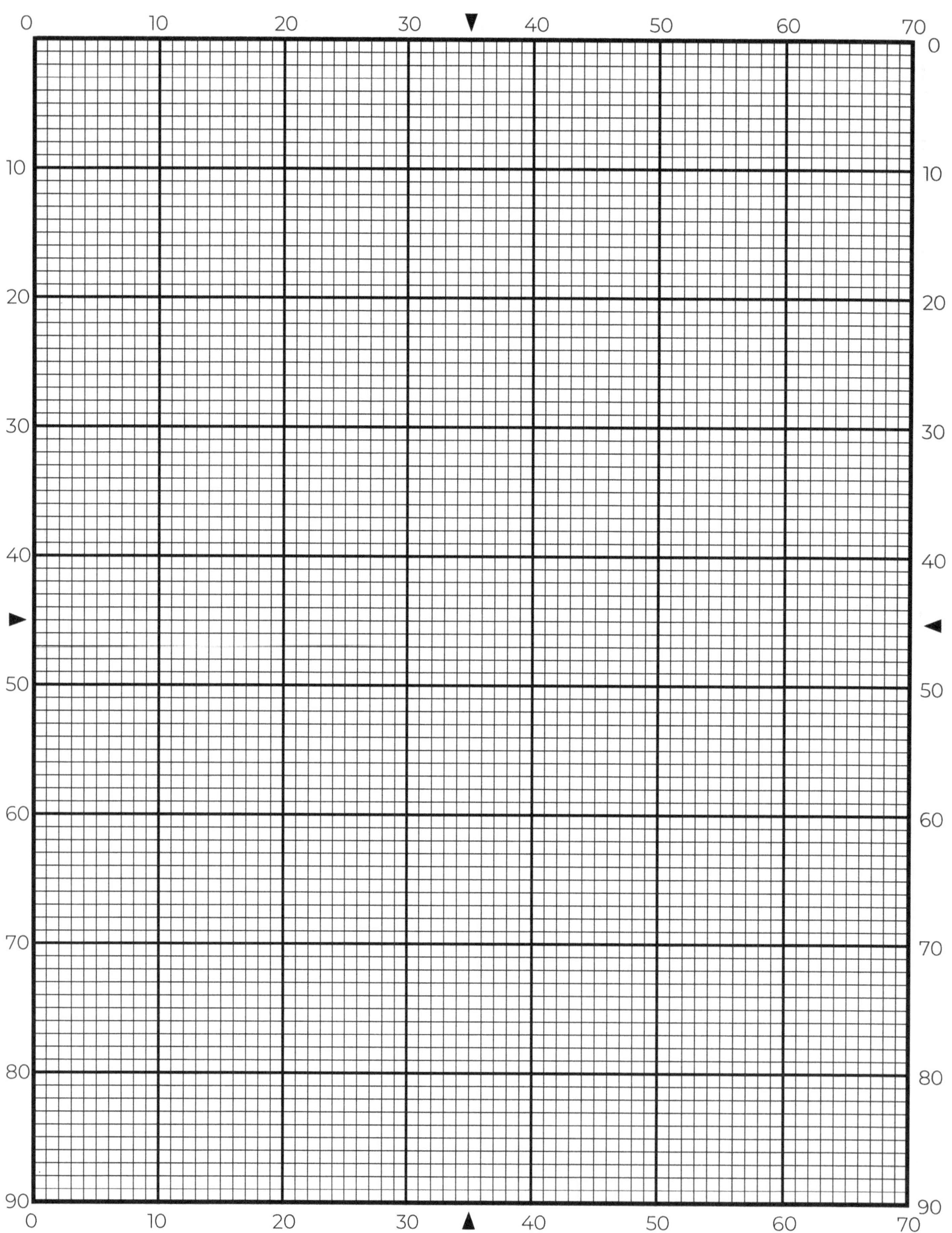

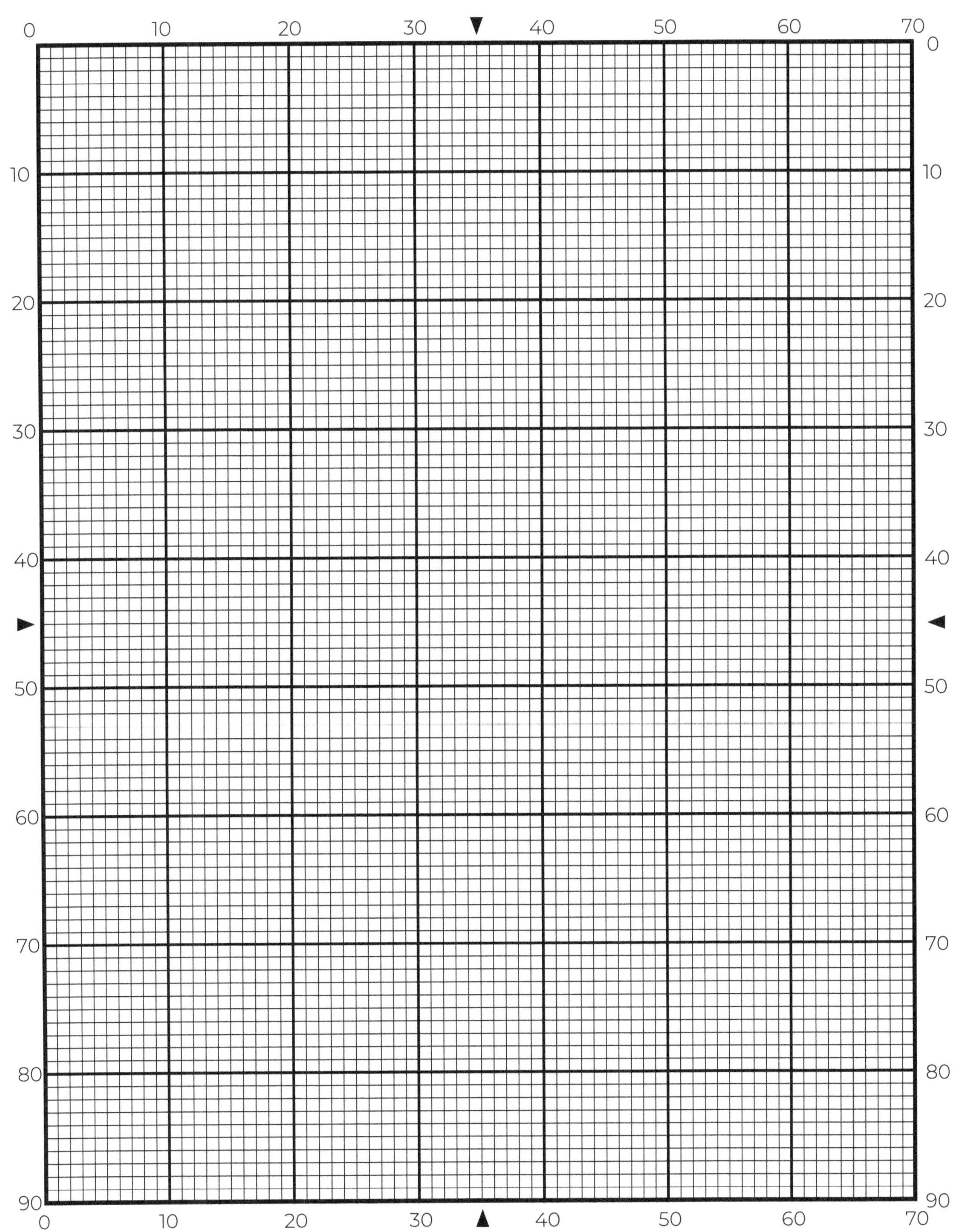

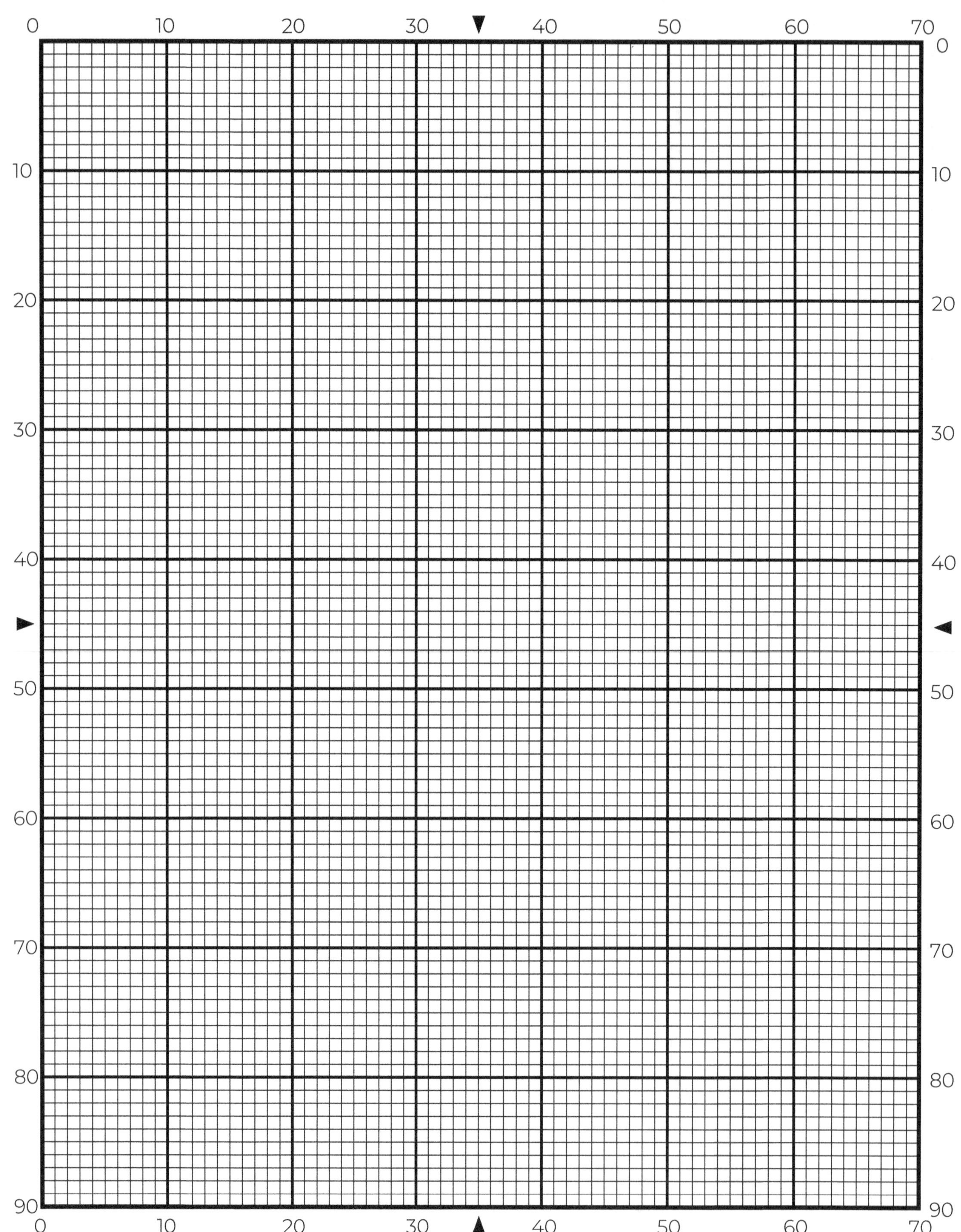

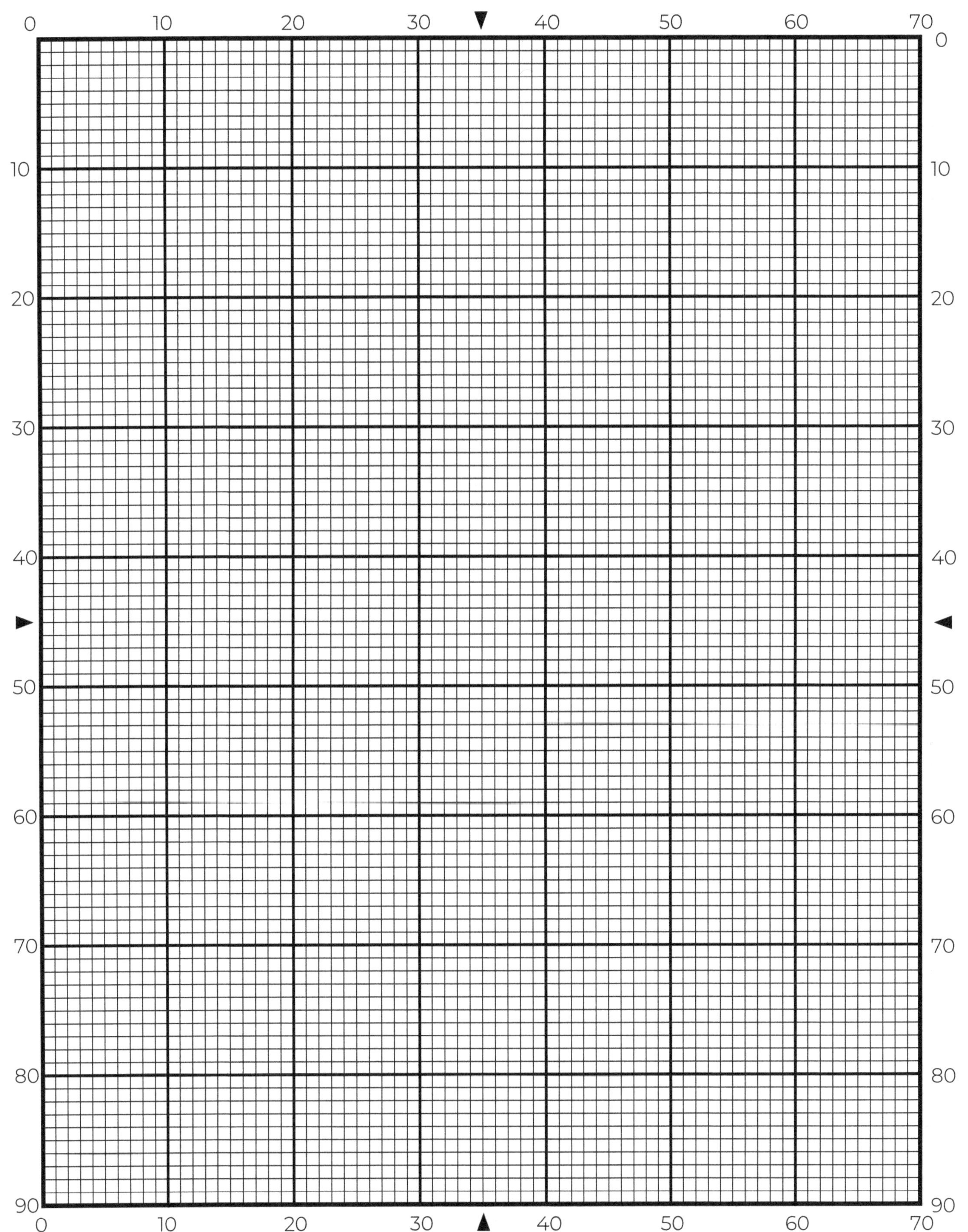

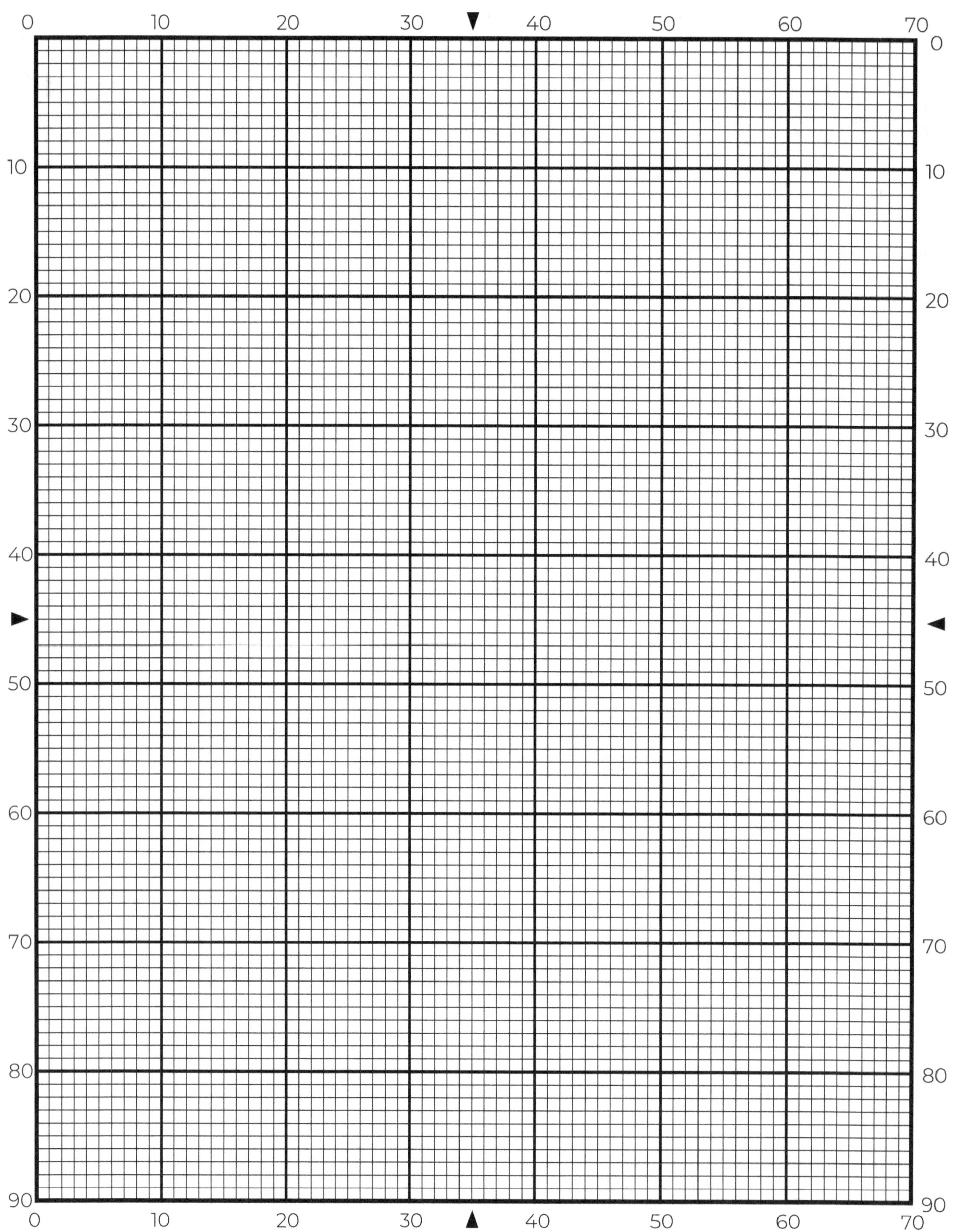

www.ingramcontent.com/pod-product-compliance
Lightning Source LLC
Chambersburg PA
CBHW080331030726
47593CB00010B/2970